Language, Gender and Parenthood Online

Language, Gender and Parenthood Online explores the digital interactions of parents on the UK-based internet discussion forum Mumsnet Talk, a space dominated by users sharing a common identification as women, parents and mothers. Using a qualitative approach grounded in feminist poststructuralist theory, Jai Mackenzie uncovers 'common-sense' assumptions about gender and parenthood, explores the construction of gender and parenthood in digital contexts and how discourses of gendered parenthood are negotiated, resisted and subverted. This is key reading for students, scholars and researchers in the field of language and gender, as well as language and digital communication.

Jai Mackenzie is a British Academy Postdoctoral Fellow at the University of Nottingham. Her primary research interests lie in explorations of language, gender, sexuality and parenthood, especially in new media contexts.

Routledge Focus on Language and Social Media
Editors: Sirpa Leppänen and Caroline Tagg

Designed for socially oriented researchers with an interest in language and technology, this series covers innovative and in-depth studies of communication through and around social media. The series takes a broad and inclusive approach, which recognizes the rapid expansion of the field, due not only to the recent proliferation of social media platforms and the increasing reach of the internet across our working, social and personal lives, but also to broadening interpretations of what both 'language' and 'social media' entail, including growing recognition of the multiple modes used alongside language, and the embedding of social media in our everyday lives. *Language and Social Media* publishes studies concerned with a wide range of relevant issues and concerns. These include but are not limited to the following:

- Identity work; identity trouble
- Constructing and debating belonging, communality, relations and networks
- Sharing, collaboration and participation
- Discourse trajectories and recontextualizations
- Complexity, diversities and differences
- Governance, surveillance and control of/in social media activities and interactions
- Digital literacies and informal learning
- Creativity and play
- Affect and attachment
- Language and social media in commercial and professional practices
- Media/language ideologies
- The wider roles of social media in the lives of individuals, groups and communities.

Language, Gender and Parenthood Online
Negotiating Motherhood in Mumsnet Talk
Jai Mackenzie

www.routledge.com/Routledge-Focus-on-Language-and-Social-Media/
book-series/LSM

Language, Gender and Parenthood Online

Negotiating Motherhood
in Mumsnet Talk

Jai Mackenzie

Routledge
Taylor & Francis Group

LONDON AND NEW YORK

First published 2019 by Routledge

2 Park Square, Milton Park, Abingdon, Oxon, OX14 4RN

605 Third Avenue, New York, NY 10017

Routledge is an imprint of the Taylor & Francis Group, an informa business

First issued in paperback 2020

British Library Cataloguing-in-Publication Data
A catalogue record for this book is available from the British
Library

Library of Congress Cataloging-in-Publication Data
A catalog record for this book has been requested

ISBN: 978-1-138-50622-0 (hbk)
ISBN: 978-0-367-73377-3 (pbk)

Typeset in Times New Roman
by Apex CoVantage, LLC

This book is dedicated to Liz Mackenzie, who showed me that there are many ways of being a good mother.

Contents

Acknowledgements

I would first like to thank Judith Baxter, who supervised the doctoral research on which this book is based, and continued to offer her support and informal mentorship beyond my graduation. Judith questioned and challenged my thinking in a way that was supportive and constructive and always pushed me to develop my ideas and writing one step further. It fills me with great sadness that she will never be able to read this book. I hope I did her proud. I would also like to thank Ruth Page, who in many ways has taken over this mentorship role, both formally and informally, and given me a great deal of her time and expertise. Thank you to the numerous people who read and offered detailed, thoughtful and constructively critical feedback on draft chapters: Caroline Tagg, Sirpa Leppänen, Ruth Page (again), Joe Bennett, Matteo Fuoli and Nick Groom. Thanks also to Laura Coffey-Glover for your friendship and companionship whilst we finished our books. Writing sessions with you made everything bearable!

Special thanks go to the Mumsnet users who allowed me to reproduce their posts, originally written with quite a different audience in mind, in the Mumsnet study. Thanks particularly to BertieBotts and freespirit, whose generous engagement with my research cannot be underestimated in the development of my approach to internet research ethics. I would also like to thank Mumsnet for giving permission to use these posts, as well as the Mumsnet logo. Aspects of the analyses and discussion originally published in Mackenzie (2017a, 2018) are reproduced with the permission of SAGE publications and Equinox Publishing Ltd, respectively. Full details of these articles are presented ahead.

Finally, thank you to my family: Roger, Hamish, Lyra, Dad, Mum and Barbara, for your unfailing love and support. You are the best.

Permission for reproduction of analysis and discussion from journal articles:

Mackenzie, J. ' "Can we have a child exchange?" Constructing and subverting the "good mother" through play in Mumsnet Talk', *Discourse & Society*, 28(3), pp. 296–312, © SAGE publications (2017), https://doi. org/10.1177/0957926516687417

Mackenzie, J. ' "Good mums don't, apparently, wear make-up": Negotiating discourses of gendered parenthood in Mumsnet Talk', *Gender and Language*, 12(1), pp. 114–135, © Equinox Publishing Ltd (2018), https:// doi.org/10.1558/genl.31062

1 Introduction

My memories of the first weeks of my son's life are hazy, but there is one that remains crystal clear. It was the middle of the night. He wouldn't sleep. He was crying relentlessly (no one had told us how much babies cry). My husband and I were taking shifts, a few hours each, and it was my turn. I put him in a sling, strapped close to my chest, and turned to the friend who has been there for me in many an hour of need. The internet. Fog-eyed and exhausted, I asked my friend those naïve questions that I'm sure many have asked before me and will ask long after. 'Why won't our baby sleep?' 'How do I stop him crying?' The top result always took me to the same place: Mumsnet. I quickly learned that the discussion forum of this popular parenting website was a font of knowledge for a fretful, sleep deprived, internet-addicted new parent like me.

I would come across Mumsnet many more times over the next few years, including in the British news media, where it has been variously described as a supportive forum based on a 'community philosophy' (McVeigh, 2012) and a 'lifeline' for its users (Duerden, 2013), yet also a 'coven of poisonous women' (Sibary, 2013) with an 'anti-male agenda' (Edmondson, 2012). My own explorations of Mumsnet have led me to feel that this site can have an overwhelmingly positive impact on the lives of its users, who come to it for many different reasons: to share advice or get information, to make friends, or just to vent their frustrations. Crucially, I felt that this was a space where women could voice, discuss and often resist some of the socio-cultural norms and expectations around being a woman and a parent – a *mother* – and in some cases to negotiate new norms of their own. This book aims to show whether that is the case through close linguistic analysis of interactions from Mumsnet's discussion forum, *Mumsnet Talk*. It explores the particular norms that seem to be relevant for Mumsnet users, and the mechanisms by which they are both taken up and negotiated. In doing so, it contributes to knowledge across the social sciences about what it means to be a parent and a mother in a digital age, as well as the theoretical and methodological strategies that can be used to uncover these insights.

Mumsnet is a well-known British website, which claims to be 'by parents, for parents' (Figure 1.1). Despite the use of the gender-neutral 'parent' in its tagline, however, the title of the site quite explicitly targets users who identify themselves as *female* parents: as *mums*. Its logo, which seems to depict three women in *Charlie's Angels*-style 'battle' poses, armed with children or feeding equipment (Figure 1.1), suggests that the site both brings together and empowers women specifically. Mumsnet users are united by a collective interest in parenthood, and they tend to share common backgrounds and identities, especially in relation to gender, class, age and sexuality. For example, demographic data (Pedersen and Smithson, 2013; Pedersen, 2016) suggests that members of Mumsnet are predominantly middle-aged working mothers, and that most have a household income above the national average and a university degree. They are also, it seems, brought together by a desire to share and connect with others. Mumsnet hosts over 6 million unique visitors each month (Pedersen, 2016) and its endorsement is highly sought after in commercial and political arenas. For example, the site

Figure 1.1 Mumsnet logo, from www.mumsnet.com, accessed 9 June 2016[1]

has hosted a number of online discussions with politicians and *The Times* described the 2010 election as the 'Mumsnet election', due to its perceived influence amongst mothers as a key voting group (Pedersen and Smithson, 2013). The evident popularity and status of Mumsnet mean that interactions in this space are likely to be influential in terms of wider ideas and expectations surrounding parenting and motherhood.

The discussion forum of the Mumsnet website, known as *Talk*, is an interactive space in which contributors can share details of their daily lives, make pleas for and offers of support and exchange ideas or information. Anyone with internet access can read interactions within this forum. Membership is only required should a visitor wish to contribute, and even then, joining is a relatively simple process. Despite Mumsnet Talk being quite a public forum, its users carefully preserve their anonymity, and the discussions that take place in this context can be surprisingly frank and intimate. This forum therefore offers relatively open access to a space where different perspectives and versions of motherhood may be expressed and explored, and may even be at the forefront of new and innovative concepts of what it means to be a 'mother'. For these reasons, it provides fruitful ground for examining the options for self-expression that are available to a particular group of women who are parents.

The importance of parenthood as a site of social regulation, inequality and conflict has been widely acknowledged in academic, and especially sociological, research. This extensive body of literature has shown that a narrow set of ideals shapes and restricts what it means to be a 'parent' in gender-specific ways: that mothers are expected to be 'natural' nurturers who are completely devoted to, and act as the primary carers for, their children (Hays, 1996; Miller, 2007; Wall, 2010, 2013), whilst fathers are assumed to be secondary, 'part-time' parents who devote most of their energies to other aspects of their lives (Miller, 2011; Sunderland, 2000, 2004). In recent years, many scholars exploring these themes have turned their attention to what a growing number of internet parenting sites such as Mumsnet (Jensen, 2013), and comparable sites around the world such as Hong Kong's 'Happy Land' (Chan, 2008) and Canada's 'Momstown' (Mulcahy, Parry and Glover, 2015), can reveal about the ways in which expressions and norms of parenting and motherhood are being taken up, negotiated and challenged in a digital age. This book is situated at the forefront of an emerging body of work that explores gender and parenthood online from a *linguistic* perspective (e.g. Hanell and Salö, 2017; Jaworska, 2017; Mackenzie, 2017a, 2018). It is the first of its kind to bring together the themes of language, gender, parenthood and digital interaction. Through close linguistic analysis of online discussions within a popular and influential forum, Mumsnet Talk, I show what kinds of social norms and expectations are relevant to parents, and especially mothers, in a contemporary British context, and consider the implications of these expectations for all kinds of parents and carers. I also examine new and potentially transformative conceptions of parenthood, and consider how their expression may be facilitated and/or constrained by the affordances of digital contexts.

A commitment to feminist poststructuralist discourse theory distinguishes this book from other research both on gender and parenthood more widely, and language, gender and parenthood online specifically. Feminist poststructuralist approaches are under-utilized in discourse studies and applied linguistics, but this book demonstrates their relevance, showing how they can support the interrogation and disruption of 'common-sense' assumptions about gender and parenthood, and help to uncover the multiple and competing perspectives that can contribute to these meanings. It shows how our understanding of gender and parenthood is governed by *discourses*, which are defined here as regulatory practices that constitute the social world, especially notions of truth, reality and knowledge: our sense of *the way things are* (Foucault, 1972, 1978). Ways of positioning ourselves in terms of family relations are also constituted through and restricted by discourses, thus limiting who it is possible to 'be' – the *subject positions* that are available to us – as well as what it is possible to 'know'. This book aims to capture key insights about how women negotiate their parental identities in relation to wider social forces in a digital age by identifying specific discourses at play in Mumsnet users' interactions, and considering how parental subject positions, such as mother, father and parent, are expressed, defined and negotiated in relation to these discourses. Chapter 2 explains these aims in more detail, in relation to the key theoretical concepts that underpin feminist poststructuralism. It also outlines some discourses of gender, parenting and motherhood that have been identified through previous sociological and sociolinguistic research to date.

Continuing with the feminist poststructuralist theme of identifying and potentially disrupting dominant social forces, Chapter 3 explores the question of whether internet discussion forums such as Mumsnet Talk can provide spaces and opportunities for the negotiation, subversion or resistance of dominant norms in society; or indeed, whether at times they may actually work to promote and perpetuate such norms, thus restricting individuals' access to multiple subject positions. This chapter also explains what existing scholarship has revealed about the ways in which gender and parenthood have been constructed and negotiated in digital contexts, and what this book adds to that scholarship. From Chapter 4, the focus shifts towards the empirical research on which this book is based. This chapter provides a transparent account of the research process, showing how a range of methodological resources drawn from ethnography, grounded theory and linguistic discourse analysis can be harnessed in the identification and analysis of discourses at both theoretical and linguistic levels. Through this detailed account of a systematic approach to identifying and analyzing discourses, it makes a significant methodological contribution to the field of discourse studies. Chapter 4 also offers a frank account of my own situation as both researcher and mother, a position that is apparent from the very opening lines of this book. It details the ways in which a self-reflexive, open and flexible approach led to the development of my situation as both insider *and* outsider in the Mumsnet community, and gave rise to sensitive, nuanced analyses of interactions from this context. It also explores the ethical concerns that were negotiated as part of the Mumsnet study, and promotes a self-reflexive, context-sensitive approach to the design of internet research.

The specific discourses that are identified through analysis of Mumsnet Talk interactions are outlined in Chapter 5. This chapter highlights the finding that discourses of gendered parenthood are dominant and powerful in Mumsnet Talk, persistently working to position parents in gendered subject positions, as *mothers* and *fathers*, often in restrictive ways. Chapter 6 explores some of the resources that Mumsnet users are able to deploy in order to negotiate, resist and subvert these discourses. It shows that the collective voice of the Mumsnet community can be a powerful force for the negotiation and challenge of dominant discourses, and the construction of 'new' norms. However, it is also suggested that this collective voice can constrain Mumsnet users, limiting their access to different ways of being an individual and a parent.

As it progresses, this book shows what it means to be a 'parent' and a 'mother' for users of Mumsnet Talk, and what discourses are at play as they negotiate their own position in relation to larger social structures and practices. It points to the importance of an emerging field of language, gender and parenthood online, showing what research in this area can reveal both about social norms and expectations around gender and parenthood, and about everyday interactions that take place in digital contexts. This book also demonstrates the value of a feminist poststructuralist approach in this kind of research, as a theoretical paradigm that facilitates close analysis of the ways in which multiple meanings surrounding gender, parenthood and identity are made and unmade in local contexts, with an eye to wider social forces. The following chapter introduces this theoretical paradigm more fully and explores its relevance to the Mumsnet study in detail.

Note

1 This logo is reproduced with the permission of Mumsnet Limited.

2 Analyzing language, gender and parenthood online

A feminist poststructuralist approach

On Mother's Day in 2014, I vented online about what I felt were the 'mothering commandments' raining down on me on this significant date in my calendar: 'I'm always there for my children, I'm told. I've nurtured them, supported them, picked them up from school, cleaned the house, cooked their tea, washed their clothes'. I wrote the blog post, felt better and carried on with my life.

Towards the end of that year, whilst exploring a Mumsnet thread titled 'Your identity as a mother' (which is introduced more fully in Chapter 4), I began to reflect on how I had positioned myself and, importantly, the *father* of my children, in this Mother's Day post. One thing I noticed about the 'Your identity as a mother' thread was that fathers were almost completely absent from Mumsnet users' narratives, and that those who *did* mention fathers, or indeed any other carer involved in their children's lives, stood out. I noticed that most authors of these posts almost exclusively employed first-person singular pronouns to position themselves in relation to their children and implied, in doing so, that they had total responsibility for those children (these insights are further detailed and explained in Chapter 5). Of course, what I came to realize was that I often did exactly the same thing when I spoke or wrote about my own family. And I had written evidence, in the form of my blog post, where I too had almost exclusively employed first-person singular pronouns to position myself in relation to my children. I had written the post as if my husband and father of our children, who is very much present in our lives, didn't exist at all.

Reflecting on my own writing online in relation to my developing analysis of *others'* writing online led to some transformative moments. For example, when I saw that the collective erasure of men and fathers from descriptions of family life was reinforcing the norm that mothers are the main parents and fathers are secondary, or even absent and completely irrelevant (I say more about these norms, or *discourses*, later in this chapter and in Chapter 5), I began to follow the lead of a small number of contributors to the 'Your identity as a mother' thread, who tended to use plural pronouns such as 'we', 'our' and 'us' when describing and naming their family. This simple difference in pronoun choice brought fathers into the family sphere and positioned them on a more equal footing with mothers. This anecdote shows how the smallest of words can perform a transformative function. It shows that a simple change from 'I' to 'we' can represent a moment of resistance and struggle against a perceived norm, and that one individual's (or group's) linguistic choices can make alternative means of expression available to others.

This chapter is devoted to an explication of the feminist poststructuralist framework that underpins this book, and that led me to uncover moments of transformation and resistance, such as the one detailed earlier. In the pages that follow, I show what research in the social sciences has revealed about the kinds of ideals, assumptions and expectations that pervade parents' lives, and how these social forces can be conceptualized, from a feminist poststructuralist perspective, as 'discourses'. I highlight the lack of theoretical rigour in much gender and parenthood research to date, which has led to a lack of clarity about what exactly is meant by, for example, 'discourses of motherhood'. I also show how such 'discourses' can operate and, importantly, how they might be challenged. The chapter closes by pointing to the need for a more explicitly theoretical and language-focused approach to naming and analyzing the social forces at play in parents' lives. This will prepare the ground for the approach that is taken in this book, which will be further detailed in Chapter 4.

Feminism, poststructuralism and feminist poststructuralism

Feminist poststructuralism offers a framework through which commonsense assumptions about gender and parenthood can be identified and brought into question, by drawing attention to the powerful, but ultimately unstable, discursive forces that constitute these norms. It can also support an exploration of the multiple ways in which individuals may position themselves, or be positioned, in relation to these norms. In order to appreciate the nature of feminist poststructuralist theory, I first briefly address its core components: *feminism* and *poststructuralism*.

The concept of feminism in a western context originates with the suffragette movement, which emerged in the late nineteenth century in the UK and US (Mills and Mullany, 2011). This movement sought to address institutional inequalities between men and women, focusing on women's right to vote. A concern to emancipate women as 'victims of a patriarchal system' (Jule, 2008: 9) has remained central to many forms of feminism, yet this goal has been problematized in recent years. Both the concept of a patriarchy, a social system that 'operates in the interests and benefit of men' (Mills and Mullany, 2011: 14), and emancipation, the movement to liberate individuals who are oppressed within such systems, construe men, women and relations between them as universal and stable. Such a conceptualization of gender relations can gloss over the complexity of gender identities, which are often not experienced as fixed *or* binary. Unidirectional concepts of gender and power can also make it difficult to appreciate the way that *multiple* axes, such as gender, class, race and age, converge and interrelate to shape power relations in society (Collins and Bilge, 2016). Positioning the central aim of feminism as the emancipation of women from a patriarchal system may therefore arguably make it *more* difficult to question, challenge and transform gender relations, because it relies on their fixedness as a central point for contestation (Baxter, 2003; Mills and Mullany, 2011). A poststructuralist perspective offers different ways of conceptualizing feminism that are able to move beyond binary gender and fixed, single-axis structures, towards the identification and disruption of more complex and intersectional power relations.

Poststructuralism has been described as the theoretical branch of postmodernism (Butler, 2002). By contrast with modernism, which seeks to emphasize permanence, stability and homogeneity (Clarke, 2003), postmodernism embraces a spirit of openness, possibility and multiplicity, in which 'things could always be otherwise' (Clarke, 2003: 560). The same foundational principles bind the diverse theories collectively known as 'poststructuralism'. One key facet that distinguishes poststructuralist from postmodernist theory, however, is its attention to language and meaning, which can be attributed largely to the influence of Saussure (1974). Saussure established poststructuralism's founding insight that language, rather than merely labelling and organizing reality, actually constitutes that reality (Weedon, 1997). Where poststructuralism departs from the structuralism of Saussure, however, is in its rejection of the notion that language can be understood as a pre-determined, fixed bank of signifiers: what Saussure (1974) calls *langue*. Instead, poststructuralists tend to see language as a social phenomenon that is plural, heterogeneous and ever-changing in nature, and as a vehicle through which dominant social norms can be resisted and transformed (Weedon, 1997). Given this central concern with language, society and meaning, it is not surprising that many linguists who are interested in social constructs such as sexuality, gender, ethnicity and class, and the intersections between them, have taken a broadly poststructuralist stance in their explorations of both popular assumptions about and individual negotiations of these constructs (e.g. Fought, 2006; Jones, 2018; Zimman, 2014).

The development of *feminist* poststructuralist theory, which integrates poststructuralist principles and feminist concerns, has been heavily influenced by the work of Michel Foucault (especially 1972, 1978) and Mikhail Bakhtin (especially 1981). A Foucauldian perspective brings to feminist poststructuralism an appreciation that, whilst social life is complex, heterogeneous and replete with possibilities, and whilst meaning is shifting and unstable, there are powerful forces that work to fix meaning; to construct the social world in specific ways. These forces are conceptualized by Foucault (1972) as *discourses*: as regulated groups of statements that restrict the ways in which we are able to see the world, and our sense of who we are. Bakhtin (1981) also scrutinizes the operation of power through regulated statements, which he calls 'languages', and highlights the difficulty of expressing oneself outside of these statements. As well as emphasizing the power of discourses, both Foucault and Bakhtin underline the potential for individual resistance, subversion and creative manipulation of these forces. This emphasis on multiplicity, resistance and challenge within dominant regulatory frameworks is important for feminist poststructuralist theory because it supports the emergence of diverse, new or transformative meanings and ways of being an individual that break away from dominant gender norms. A central goal of feminist poststructuralism is to disrupt and transform existing power relations, in order to open up 'all social ways of being to all people' (Weedon, 1997: 18).

There has been some disagreement, however, as to whether poststructuralist theory can adequately serve feminist interests. Feminist scholars such as Gill (1995), for example, have argued that the two movements are incompatible because poststructuralism withdraws from the stable, unified identities, generalizations and global concerns that have been so important for feminism and other political activism. Poststructuralist theorists such as Baxter (2003), however, have questioned whether the homogenization and universal emancipation of large groups, which are actually quite diverse and heterogenous, is a useful goal. A feminist poststructuralist approach offers a different perspective, one that focuses on the fluid, unstable and contested meanings surrounding power, gender and identity (Baxter, 2003). It can support the interrogation of constructs such as gender, sexuality and identity themselves; the questioning of what it means to be, for example, a woman or a man, both or neither, straight, gay or bisexual, feminine or masculine, and how our understanding of such concepts is regulated by discourses (Mills and Mullany, 2011; Weedon, 1997). It can facilitate an exploration of how discourses work to fix meanings around gender, sexuality and identity, and position individual subjects in relation to these meanings, but also how individuals might negotiate and shape these discourses, defining and redefining for themselves the practices through which they are positioned

(Weedon, 1997). The political, interrogative and transformative goals of feminist poststructuralism drive the aims of this book: to identify the dominant social forces that may work to fix and restrict the options that are available to parents, and to explore the ways in which such forces may be reinforced, and/or disrupted, in a digital context.

Discourses, gender and parenthood

Discourses are treated in this book as *constitutive practices*, drawing from Foucault's (1972: 42) definition of discourses as 'practices that systematically form the objects of which they speak'. This definition captures the powerful capacity of discourses to constitute and shape social meanings and realities. A central nexus of knowledge, power and subjectivity (Angermuller, Maingueneau and Wodak, 2014) makes discourses different from, say, 'themes' or 'ideas'. Themes, for example, share with discourses the property of being a set of recurring statements. That group of statements is a discourse, however, only if it constitutes knowledge, positions subjects and inscribes power relations – if it regulates our sense of who we are, what we know and the power to define that knowledge and subjectivity. Subjectivity is defined here as the condition of being subject to, positioned or regulated by discursive frameworks (Skeggs, 1997), whilst subject *positions* are defined as the 'ways of being an individual' (Weedon, 1997: 3) that are made available by specific discourses. The subject position 'mother', for example, is of particular interest here. The concept of subjectivity relates closely to the key aims of this book: to explore the ways in which users of Mumsnet Talk are able to position themselves in relation to wider discourses, and to consider what these insights reveal about the options that are available to parents outside of this specific domain.

In keeping with the principles of feminist poststructuralist theory, the relations between knowledge, power and subjectivity are understood in this book to be plural and competing (Baxter, 2003), and discourses as constantly shifting in relation to one another (Foucault, 1978). Baxter's (2003) exploration of interactions between students, as part of an English GCSE speaking and listening assignment, provides an illustration of the potential complexity of these relations. In her comparison of the discursive interplay of power and subjectivity between two female students, for example, she shows how one is positioned as relatively powerful in relation to the discourse of teacher approval, but relatively powerless in relation to peer approval, because approval by the teacher is perceived as 'boffiness', and 'boffins' are generally not as popular with their peers. Both students, due to their adoption of a collaborative, supportive, interactional style in discussions with their peers, are positioned as reasonably powerful in relation to the discourse of collaborative talk, which is highly valued in the speaking and listening assessment criteria. At the same time, Baxter (2003) suggests, this power might be diminished within a discourse of gender differentiation, which constitutes female interlocutors as inherently good listeners, thus de-emphasizing any personal skill or effort on the students' part. Baxter's (2003) analysis is a good example of the way that, rather than being dominated by singular and powerful forces at all times, a complex interplay of knowledge, power and subjectivity constitutes human experience. Thus, some discourses, and the subjects they produce, may be relatively powerful at one moment, but relatively powerless at another; they may also be simultaneously powerful *and* powerless (Baxter, 2003).

Despite the inevitable interplay between discourses, however, some discourses gain the status and currency of 'truth' at a particular time, or in a particular context. Such discourses can become synonymous with popular conceptions of what is 'everyday' or 'normal', acquiring a 'very special kind of obviousness' that comes to be seen as just 'common sense' – the way things more or less unavoidably *are* (Althusser, 1971: 139). Discourses that have acquired such common-sense legitimacy can be described as dominant, because they are likely to dominate the ways in which individuals are able to define and organize both themselves and the social world around them, and work to marginalize other ways of understanding the world. It can be difficult to think, act, speak or position oneself in the world outside of such dominant discourses.

The popular, 'common-sense' view that men and women are two homogeneous and distinct groups, and the subsequent constitution of gendered subject positions such as 'mother', 'father', 'daughter' and 'son', can be understood, in discourse-theoretical terms, as produced by a dominant, pervasive collection of discourses that position men and women as fundamentally *distinct* and *different*. Researchers in the field of gender and language have identified and named this set of discourses as, variously, 'discourses of gender difference' (Baker, 2008: 107), 'discourses of gender differentiation' (Baxter, 2003: 36), or 'gendered discourses' (Sunderland, 2004: 3). These labels all utilize the plural form, thus foregrounding the multiplicity of discourses that constitute binary gender relations. In addition, Baker (2008) and Baxter (2003) both underline the way these relations rely on the key component of *difference*. 'Gender differentiation', as it will be named herein, can be described as the nexus of a group of intersecting discourses, or in Sunderland's (2000: 261) terms, as an 'overarching' discourse, that can both exist independently of and incorporate a range of other discourses.

Identifying and analyzing discourses of gender differentiation has allowed researchers of gender and language to draw attention to the profoundly gendered nature of the social world, and to name some of the specific ways in which gendered meanings are produced. For example, Sunderland (2004: 150) identifies the complementary discourses 'father as mother's bumbling assistant' and 'mother as manager of the father's role in childcare' in parentcraft texts. She also identifies a gendered 'division of labour' discourse, which positions men as heads of the household, and women as 'inside-the-house people', in American award-winning children's books. Sunderland's (2004) work points to the many ways in which gender inequalities and discriminatory practices, such as excluding fathers from the role of main parent and excluding women from the workforce, are enabled through restrictive gendered discourses. The fixed, dichotomous positions that are offered by discourses of gender differentiation make it very difficult for individuals to position themselves outside of the gender binary, with all the cultural assumptions that come with it, even though these assumptions may be problematic.

Researchers of gender and parenthood across the social sciences have also identified a number of discourses of gender differentiation (although they do not tend to name them as such) that work to fix individuals who are parents in restrictive gendered subject positions. This body of research focuses primarily on western, English-speaking contexts, with the studies mentioned ahead taking place in the US, Britain and Canada. Lowe (2016: 40), for example, points to a dominant discourse of intensive motherhood, which 'requires that women invest time and resources into a child-centred model of mothering in order to ensure that their children reach their full potential'. Within this framework, women are positioned as natural nurturers, and therefore mothers as the obvious primary carers for their children. The significance of 'intensive motherhood', which Lowe (2016) and Wall (2013) call a discourse but is introduced by Hays (1996) as a model, is well documented in sociological research, with many suggesting that it not only persists (Lawler, 2000; Miller, 2007) but also continues to intensify (Johnston and Swanson, 2006, 2007; Wall, 2010, 2013). The imperative for mothers to be child-centred (to put children first in all they do) is the cornerstone of 'intensive motherhood'. This discourse is therefore closely linked with a discourse of 'child-centredness'. Wall (2010, 2013) has suggested that the demands placed upon mothers to be child-centred have intensified in recent years; that mothers are now expected to be both expert in and entirely responsible for the early development and future success of their children. Her study of twenty-first-century articles from a Canadian parenting magazine (Wall, 2013) shows how discourses of intensive child-centred mothering, neoliberal self-responsibility and risk converge in a way that makes it difficult for women to legitimize their other needs whilst also positioning themselves as 'good mothers'. She suggests that the convergence of these discourses has a powerful effect, working to 'open up less rather than more space for women's equality in the workplace and family' (Wall, 2013: 170).

The expectation that women will both devote themselves completely to their children *and* participate fully in the workforce gives rise to what Hays (1996) calls the irreconcilable 'cultural contradiction' of motherhood in western cultures. In Ennis's (2014: 333) review of the future of 'intensive mothering', she argues that this contradiction continues to cause 'enormous ambivalence for mothers', because they are unable to adequately fulfil both expectations. Further, in Takševa's (2014: 229) account of how mothering practices are increasingly shaped by consumerism, she suggests that the nurturing, selfless qualities of the 'intensive mother' and a capitalist socio-economic system based on competition are becoming more and more interrelated; that the ways in which mothers express love for their children are 'increasingly defined by their active and willing participation in consumer culture'. She offers as an example the expectation that 'good' mothers will provide a range of enrichment activities for their children from a young age, such as mother-and-baby programmes, ballet classes and French-immersion camps. This emphasis on the expensive 'enrichment' of children's lives and opportunities through the exchange of goods and services, she suggests, reinforces the privileged, middle class values at the heart of both 'intensive motherhood' and the concept of 'good motherhood' in general (see Gillies, 2007; Hays, 1996; Lawler, 2000; Miller, 2007; Wall, 2010).

Research exploring constructions and representations of *fathers* (e.g. Miller, 2011; Sunderland, 2000, 2004) has tended to suggest that discourses of fatherhood contrast sharply with discourses of motherhood. For example, Sunderland's (2000: 257) analysis of parentcraft texts (to which I return in the following section) led her to identify 'part-time father/mother as main parent' as a 'combination discourse' that captures the oppositionality of discourses around fatherhood and motherhood. The discourses of fatherhood that she identifies are quite striking for their lack of emphasis on responsibility and 'natural' inclinations. The 'part-time father' discourse, for example, positions fathers in an essentially 'supporting and non-responsible role' (Sunderland, 2000: 258). Sunderland also identifies three specific discourses that support this overarching 'part-time father' discourse: 'father as baby entertainer', 'father as mother's bumbling assistant' and 'father as line manager'. Conversely, Miller's (2011) study of men's narratives around first-time fatherhood (which mirrors her 2007 study of mothers) suggests that emerging discourses such as 'involved fatherhood' enable fathers to position themselves beyond these limiting roles – for example as caring, intimate, emotional and taking an equal role in the care of their children. However, Miller (2011: 1096) also points to the continued division between gendered parental roles, arguing that discourses of fatherhood, by contrast with discourses of motherhood, 'do not invoke biological predisposition'. Discourses of fatherhood and motherhood can therefore be said to feed into a dominant, overarching discourse of gender differentiation that positions men and women as separate and fundamentally different kinds of parents.

Most of the research that has been mentioned so far explores social forces relating to gender and parenthood from a broadly poststructuralist perspective. It often uses the concept of discourses to capture and name some of the ways in which these forces operate in people's everyday lives. However, research in this area (with the exception of Sunderland's work, to which I will return in the next section) has tended to conceptualize discourses as powerful, dominant forces in parents' lives, without specifying what discourses *are*, how they operate and how they are identified, named and analyzed. For example, in her exploration of women's transition to first-time motherhood, Miller (2007) refers to 'good mothering' discourses, but she is not explicit about how specific 'good mothering' discourses may be manifested, or what subject positions they may offer. In her later study of men's transition to first-time fatherhood, Miller (2011: 1102) suggests that her participants 'invoke strands of a discourse of involved fatherhood', but never explains how she identifies these strands. Lowe (2016: 41, 28), similarly, names 'good motherhood' as an essentializing discourse, but does not explicitly detail either what she means by a discourse or whether and how a discourse is distinct from other terms she uses for regulatory forces, such as 'ideology', 'norm' or 'dominant framework'. Such broad conceptualizations of discourses have certainly been useful, because they underline dominant norms and expectations that are relevant in the lives of many parents – for example the restrictive ways in which 'good motherhood' is defined. However, vague claims about discourses and how they can be identified also contribute to a widespread lack of clarity as to what 'discourses' *are*, how they operate in everyday practice and how discursive analysis can enhance research in the social sciences generally, and studies of gender and parenthood more specifically. The following section explores this issue further by focusing on the question of *how* discourses can be identified and analyzed, with reference to insights from both sociolinguistics and discourse studies.

Identifying and analyzing discourses

Identifying and analyzing discourses is not a straightforward operation. As many critical discourse analysts have pointed out, discourses are not isolated entities; they can merge, combine and interrelate (van Leeuwen, 2009), becoming 'intimately entangled' with one another (Jäger and Maier, 2009: 35). It is likely that many discourses will come together in any given text, and in fact it may be difficult to distinguish individual discourses at all when they are heavily interconnected and intertextually linked (Baxter, 2003). This state of diverse interrelation is described by Fairclough (1992) and Sunderland (2004) as 'interdiscursivity'. Discourses are also not fixed; they are shifting and unstable, fluid and interpretive, making the boundaries of a discourse almost impossible to delimit (Reisigl and Wodak, 2009). It would seem, by these tokens, that there can be no concrete, clearly defined, easily identifiable discourses. Similarly, it would be very difficult to pinpoint all the discourses that are in circulation at any one given time. It would be like trying to count the grains of sand on a beach; before the searcher could complete their task, the sands would have shifted in unpredictable ways and individual grains would have changed shape. In a sense, analysts can immortalize discourses by identifying and writing about them. But over time, text, culture and speaker, the nature of discourses, as they operate in societal practices, will change. How discourses are seen and named will also depend on the analyst's perspective, and indeed, will tell us something about the namer, and the position from which they stand, as well as the discourses they name (Reisigl and Wodak, 2009; Sunderland, 2004).

It is perhaps because of the complex, unstable and shifting nature of discourses that the mechanisms for identifying them are so rarely made explicit in an otherwise extensive body of discourse studies literature from across the social sciences. For example, as noted earlier, sociologists exploring the theme of motherhood have pointed to a range of discourses of parenthood, such as 'good mothering' (Lowe, 2016; Miller, 2007), 'child-centredness' (Wall, 2013) and 'involved fatherhood' (Miller, 2011), without making the means by which they come to name these discourses explicit. Readers are consequently relying on the author's, as well as their own, intuitions and assumptions in order to understand what it is exactly that reveals the presence of these discourses. Intuitions may well have a place in the identification and analysis of discourses, but such analyses are unlikely to move beyond a certain level of sophistication. They are unlikely to be able to reveal very much, for example, about exactly how discursive forces operate in social practice, how they merge and combine and, importantly, how they can be negotiated and challenged.

Those who do directly address the issue of discourse identification tend, conversely, to emphasize the limitations of any effort to outline fixed methods for identifying discourses. The work of Sunderland (2000, 2004), for example, is often cited in relation to discourse identification within the field of gender and language, as well as sociolinguistics more widely, yet she insists that discourses cannot be recognized 'in any straightforward way' (Sunderland, 2004: 28). Indeed, to offer, or follow, a prescribed, definitive method for identifying discourses would in many ways be counter to poststructuralist principles, which resist prescription and claims to 'truth' or 'objectivity' through 'scientific', 'precise' methodologies (Graham, 2005: 3). However, several discourse analysts *have* offered some guidance, not by *pre*scribing specific methods but by *de*scribing their methods for discourse identification in detail.

There are a handful of discourse analysts, particularly those working from a critical perspective, who have illustrated their methods for systematically evidencing discourses through close scrutiny of language. It is through language, after all, that discursive struggles are acted out, so it makes sense that discourses can be reconstructed through close linguistic analysis (Mills, 2004; Sunderland, 2004). For example, van Leeuwen (2009) focuses on a text's representation of actors, actions, times and places, through markers such as lexical choice and verb type. Baxter (2010) examines lexical choices, turn taking and verb tense, whilst Reisigl and Wodak (2009: 93) locate what they call 'discursive strategies' in a wide range of specific linguistic devices, such as metaphor, collocation, verbs, nouns and adjectives. These discursive strategies include 'nomination', 'predication', 'argumentation', 'perspectivization' and 'intensification' (Reisigl and Wodak, 2009: 94). Several of these analysts have used visual resources, such as tables and other diagrams, to chart and compare the discursive strategies deployed in a range of texts (e.g. Reisigl and Wodak, 2009; van Leeuwen, 2009). By doing so, they can see at a glance how a particular text defines, describes or conceptualizes the topic at hand, who or what is foregrounded, and what particular forms of knowledge and subjectivity are being constructed. A range of factors have influenced these scholars' choices to emphasize particular linguistic features over others. For example, Baxter's (2010) attention to turn-taking practices is particularly appropriate for the analysis of spoken interaction. Fairclough's (1992) focus on transitivity, theme and modality reveals his commitment to the systemic functional linguistic approach. By unpacking the linguistic mechanisms through which discourses operate, these discourse analysts have revealed some of the ways in which specific discourses can be demystified, disrupted and challenged.

Sunderland's (2000, 2004) approach to identifying and analyzing gendered discourses in parentcraft texts (leaflets and books about pregnancy and childcare) has a great deal in common with the research presented in this book. Sunderland works to pinpoint specific gendered discourses by first identifying recurrences and repetitions in these texts, such as 'play', 'fun' and 'help', in line with van Leeuwen's (2009) approach to the reconstruction of discourses. For example, she suggests that the 'part-time father/ mother as main parent' discourse 'is realized through the recurrence of *help*', which is largely attributed to fathers, whilst the 'father as baby entertainer' discourse 'is realized through recurrences of *play, fun and enjoy*', again attributed largely to male parents (Sunderland, 2000: 265). Sunderland also pays attention to absences, as well as presences, in parentcraft texts, drawing again on the work of van Leeuwen (1995, 1996) in her exploration of 'what possibilities do not appear, but could have done' (Sunderland, 2000: 32). For example, the *absence* of linguistic items such as 'share' and 'paternity leave', as well as the backgrounding of fathers through lack of specific reference to men as parental subjects, contributes to her identification of the overarching 'part-time father/mother as main parent' discourse. Sunderland (2000: 255) is also influenced by grounded theory, developing emergent theory about the discourses at work in a text through close analysis of the linguistic structures that indicate their presence, so that discourses are 'both the object and the result' of her analysis.

This book can be distinguished from Sunderland's (2000, 2004) work in two important ways. First, the context for exploring the themes of language, gender and parenthood here is an online discussion forum, which has quite different dynamics from the parentcraft texts at the heart of Sunderland's research. Within Mumsnet Talk, for example, any member can create content by contributing to discussions, making it much more user-oriented than the books and leaflets that Sunderland analyzes. Second, the Mumsnet study is more firmly grounded in poststructuralist theory. Although Sunderland's work goes a good deal further than other research that identifies discourses of parenthood, her analysis at times loses sight of some of the key facets of discourses: namely their central nexus of knowledge, power and subjectivity. This is apparent in her description of discourses as 'ways of looking at the world' (Sunderland, 2000: 261), which suggests that discourses offer particular ways of seeing things, but does not capture the complex mechanisms of power that are bound up with the discursive constitution of knowledge and subjectivity. As a result, I would argue that some of the 'specific' discourses that Sunderland (2000: 268) names, such as 'father as mother's bumbling assistant' and 'mother as manager of the father's role in childcare', would be more accurately described as *themes:* as groups of ideas or values that recur in the texts she analyzes, rather than *discourses* that govern their subjects' minds and bodies (this point is also raised in Mackenzie, 2018). This book illustrates an approach that places more emphasis on the discursive nexus of knowledge, power and subjectivity, focusing more intensely on the ways in which particular linguistic items can be said to constitute forms of knowledge and position subjects, and thereby inscribe power relations. The nature of this approach is further explicated in Chapter 4.

Concluding remarks

This chapter has laid the foundations for the exploration of language, gender and parenthood online that will follow. It has outlined the origins and key concepts of the feminist poststructuralist framework that underpins this book, placing particular emphasis on the concept of 'discourses', and the kinds of insights that have been revealed about discourses of gender and parenthood to date. I have drawn particular attention to the ways in which discourses of gender differentiation, which position men and women as fundamentally distinct and different, can be problematic, for people in general, but more specifically for parents. This chapter has also emphasized the limitations of existing research that draws on poststructuralist theory to explore the themes of gender, parenthood, identity and society. The ways in which this book addresses these limitations will be further explicated in the chapters that follow. Chapter 4, for example, will detail the research design and methods employed in the Mumsnet study, showing how a language-focused, feminist poststructuralist approach can be carried out in practice. Chapter 5 will outline the discourses that are identified through this approach, specifying the nature of these discourses, the linguistic mechanisms through which they operate, and the ways in which they are taken up in everyday interactions.

Before going on to explore these discourses, Chapter 3 will pick up on the feminist poststructuralist theme of identifying and potentially disrupting dominant social forces. It will ask whether internet discussion forums such as Mumsnet Talk can provide spaces and opportunities for the negotiation, subversion or resistance of dominant norms, considering some of the ways in which digital contexts have been shown to facilitate but also constrain their users' opportunities to subvert and transgress social norms. It will also explore some of the key themes of studies that have focused on issues of gender, parenthood and identity in digital interaction, and show how this book both builds on and develops those themes.

3 Constructing gender and parenthood in digital contexts

Digital technologies are an integral part of our social lives. Research that explores how we interact, share information and communicate about our sense of self and the world around us in digital contexts therefore has an important place in the study of social phenomena. This chapter considers how the social constructs that are of most interest for this book, gender and parenthood, have been constituted and negotiated in digital contexts. In doing so, it situates this book within a growing tradition of digital discourse studies, particularly research that considers explorations of gender, parenthood and identity in digital spaces. The chapter also explains in detail what an internet discussion forum is, considering what kinds of social possibilities internet discussion forums in general, and Mumsnet Talk specifically, might afford, and what makes them such relevant and interesting sites for the exploration of language, gender and parenthood online.

Gender and identity online

Studies of sociability, interaction and identity construction in digital contexts have often had a strong allegiance with the core principles of postmodern and poststructuralist theory, conceptualizing online spaces as ideal sites for postmodern self-expressions of difference, diversity and hybridity (Georgakopoulou, 2005). Digital technologies can offer a number of *affordances* (Gibson, 1977) that facilitate such possibilities. For example, they can allow people to communicate when they are separated in time and/or space (Baron, 2008; Georgakopoulou, 2005; Seargeant and Tagg, 2014). Online interactions may therefore take place across geographical and time boundaries and, importantly, with a degree of anonymity. Such anonymity may make it possible for people to express themselves more freely, allowing them to move beyond socio-cultural expectations and constraints that would ordinarily be difficult to challenge or overcome (Benwell and Stokoe, 2006; Markham, 2004; Turkle, 1995). Barton and Lee (2013) have suggested, further, that the physical separation of interlocutors, together with the opportunity to carefully manage interactions and sharing practices, can give individuals more control over their self-presentation. Thus, they suggest, identity online can increasingly become a matter of 'who we want to be to others' (Barton and Lee, 2013: 68). This section considers the idea that digital technologies may open up possibilities for diverse self-expressions in detail. It focuses, in particular, on expressions of gendered identities, and how individuals have been shown to negotiate wider gender norms when they interact online.

Several early studies of identity, community and interaction in online role-playing games (e.g. Cherny, 1999; Danet, 2001; Turkle, 1995) have shown that players of these games have been able to move beyond fixed gendered categories and constraints to some extent. Within the online role-playing game 'LambdaMOO', for example, Cherny (1999) and Turkle (1995) report that users feel able to 'become' someone else for a sustained period, including someone of a gender that is different from the one with which they usually identify. Danet (2001) points out that LambdaMOO facilitates such flexible self-identifications by offering its users a range of pronoun categories from which to choose, including 'neuter', 'either', 'plural', 'egotistical' and 'royal', amongst many others. This game therefore facilitates users' engagement with play as a form of 'make-believe' (Goffman, 1974; Handelman, 1977), allowing them to experiment with multiple identities and possibilities (Danet, Ruedenberg-Wright and Rosenbaum-Tamari, 1997; Handelman, 1977). As one of Turkle's (1995: 184) participants puts it, 'You can be whoever you want to be. You can completely redefine yourself if you want. You can be the opposite sex. You can be more talkative. You can be less talkative. Whatever'. Such explorations of gender play and flexibility online have not been limited to role-playing games. In his study of Swiss internet relay chats, for example, Rellstab (2007) analyzes the practice of users who temporarily 'switch' their gender presentation in a playful, performative way, as where one user, *beeRee*, accepts another's miscategorization of her as a gay man, and proceeds to offer an exaggerated performance of this identity category in her subsequent posts. These brief, 'temporary transgressions', Rellstab (2007: 780) suggests, are made possible by both users' relative anonymity and, relatedly, their freedom from the usual possible consequences of such transgressions in their everyday lives.

More recent studies exploring the themes of language, gender and identity in digital contexts have tended to focus less on such explicit play with and performance of gender categories and roles, instead turning their attention to some of the ways in which individuals may take up, negotiate and potentially transgress gender norms and cultural expectations in their more everyday digital interactions. For example, Gong (2016), Hall, Gough,

Seymour-Smith and Henson (2012) and Milani (2013) explore the ways in which contributors to the Arsenal Football Club message boards on a Chinese site (*Baidu*), a thread within a US discussion forum (*MacRumors*) on the topic of metrosexuality, and a South African community for men seeking men (*meetmarket*) negotiate both hegemonic and marginalized forms of masculinity. All three studies suggest that these are rich sites for the expression and negotiation of multiple and competing masculinities. In a Finnish context, both Halonen and Leppänen (2017) and Leppänen (2008) have explored the ways in which young women negotiate different forms of femininity and sexuality in the context of fictional stories about 'pissis girls', a category that embodies 'a particular version of "bad" young femininity' (Halonen and Leppänen, 2017: 39), and stories from fan fiction sites. They suggest that these contexts offer young women a relatively safe space in which they can explore, parody, identify or disidentify with different forms of femininity and relate these explorations to their own lives and experiences. Similarly, Lehtonen's (2017) exploration of young Finnish men's stories about being a 'brony' (an adult male fan of the *My Little Pony* series, which targets young girls) reveals that the discussion forum of the Brony fansite provides them with opportunities to 'do' gender in ways that deviate from cultural norms in potentially empowering ways.

Many of the digital contexts that are mentioned earlier have affordances in common that may facilitate such diverse and multiple expressions of gender and identity. Most notably, interaction between users is a key feature of these sites. In addition, contributors to the discussion forums of sites such as Brony and MacRumors adopt pseudonymous usernames, taking advantage of the option to choose how they present themselves online, where they are physically separated from their interlocutors. They are also largely quite accessible and public sites, affordances that provide users with a platform from which they can be heard by many. Contributors to these public sites therefore have the opportunity to engage with and potentially work to transform the dominant discourses available to them in a way that may have an impact beyond their immediate social networks. As Leppänen (2008: 171) puts it, public sites offer a platform from which individuals can 'transform and change the "official" stories they have at their disposal'. A final aspect that these sites have in common is that they bring people together around a common identification or interest, and many are seen as supportive, 'safe' environments that engender a sense of belonging and community. Even Brony, for example, which Lehtonen (2017: 291) suggests 'is not a close-knit community', is perceived by its users as a 'safe space' in which they can share their thoughts and experiences openly, in a way that they do not feel is possible in other contexts. Contributors to these sites also seem to draw on similar resources and strategies to experiment with gender norms.

The negotiation of meanings around gendered categories, especially contrasting pairs, such as 'goafushuai' and 'diaosi' (Gong, 2016), 'metrosexual' and 'homosexual' (Hall et al., 2012) and 'guy' and 'man' (Milani, 2013), for example, is a common theme. Irony, parody and humour are also highlighted as important strategies for exploring, interrogating or (dis)identifying with different forms of gendered and sexual identities (Hall et al., 2012; Halonen and Leppänen, 2017; Leppänen, 2008; Milani, 2013). The importance of irony and parody as discursive resources in these contexts points to the continued relevance of *play* online: irony can be seen as play with concepts of truth and falseness (see Bateson, 1972), and parody as a form of imitative play that can involve experimentation with multiple possibilities (see Danet et al., 1997).

Despite demonstrating the opportunities that the internet can afford for innovative and potentially transformative interactions and expressions of self, many of the authors who are cited earlier have also pointed to the ways in which internet users remain constrained by dominant gender norms. Hall et al. (2012), Milani (2013) and Gong (2016), for example, suggest that discourses of hegemonic masculinity and sexism continue to influence the negotiation of supposedly 'new', 'alternative' or 'queer' forms of masculinity in the digital contexts they explore. Elm's (2007) study of the Swedish online community 'Lunarstorm', in addition, shows that the self-presentations of young contributors to this site, contrary to her expectations, largely adhere to stereotypical expectations of 'masculinity' and 'femininity' and reinforce heteronormative ideals. Jäntti, Saresma, Leppänen, Järvinen and Varis (2017) point to the 'echo chamber effect' (Sunstein, 2001) in Finnish 'homing blogs', which are written mainly by women, and tend to focus on the themes of home and family life. They suggest that this effect is created as a result of bloggers and commenters being drawn towards like-minded others, and subsequently 'echoing' one another's ideas and expressions in a monologic way. Jäntti et al. (2017: 12) suggest that this effect stifles new forms of expression, working, in this context, to 'reinforce conservative gender ideologies'. These studies show that whilst some individuals may feel more able to express themselves openly online, or to challenge dominant social norms, those norms do not disappear; indeed, in some online contexts, as elsewhere, they may be felt with particular force.

A large number of the studies that have been reviewed in this section are based around internet discussion forums (IDFs), suggesting that IDFs may be fruitful sites for challenging and experimenting with gender norms online. The next section outlines the nature of discussion forums, and parenting forums in particular, before considering whether this is the case, through further exploration of the potential opportunities and restrictions these spaces may engender.

Parenting discussion forums and Mumsnet Talk

An internet discussion forum (IDF) is usually an area of a website in which individuals create and/or add to 'threads': digital conversations that are centred around a particular topic, theme or question. IDFs can be contrasted with the edited sections of websites, which are generally controlled by owners or administrators, because they are more focused around the *user*, offering 'platforms for peer-to-peer interaction where users become an audience to their own discourse' (Androutsopoulos, 2006: 524). In this way, they are part of wider technological and social trends that have allowed users to generate content in collaborative ways (Barton and Lee, 2013; Cormode and Krishnamurthy, 2008; Zappavigna, 2012). Members of websites with discussion forums (or other content-sharing affordances) are therefore not just audiences for official, edited content, but can be seen as *produsers* (Bruns, 2008): users, producers and distributors, all at the same time. IDFs are a continuing feature of many websites that aim to bring people together, offering individuals with common interests, experiences and/or identities the opportunity to 'buil[d] bonds and reac[h] out to other interested groups' (Hall et al., 2012: 384). Although IDFs will tend to have certain key features in common, they can also vary quite significantly from one site to another. The rest of this section will therefore specifically examine the parenting discussion forum that is the focus of this book, Mumsnet Talk.

The discussion forum of the Mumsnet website, *Talk*, is divided into a large number of sub-topics (285 at the time of writing), such as nurseries, feminist activism, pets and Gransnet, so that users can choose to restrict their interactions to very specific themes, if they wish. Within Talk topics, users can post to individual threads. The sub-topic 'Chat', which is the source of data discussed in this book, can be distinguished from most others by the limited life of its threads (they are deleted 90 days after being posted) and its lack of specific topic focus. Popular threads are easy to access via the Mumsnet Talk toolbar in the top right corner of the home page, which displays selected 'active' threads, or users can search for topics that interest them.

Anyone with internet access can read Mumsnet Talk threads, making this a highly accessible forum (see Chapter 1). Nevertheless, members of Mumsnet maintain a degree of anonymity within this space by choosing pseudonymous, idiosyncratic usernames. The names of two participants in the Mumsnet study, 'cakesonatrain' and 'SheWhoDaresGins', are characteristically imaginative, witty and subversive, drawing on well-known cultural references and expressions (the film *Snakes on a Plane* and the saying 'he who dares wins'), at the same time as playing with some slightly subversive British stereotypes about mothers: that they eat a lot of cake and drink a lot of gin, mainly as a form of escapism from their demanding lives. Members also deploy a range of strategies, such as name-changing and selective sharing, to maintain their anonymity within, as well as outside of, the site (the nature of these practices and the implications in terms of research ethics are further explored in Mackenzie, 2017b). In addition, very little information about Mumsnet members is available within the site. Users can set up an individual profile page including details about themselves, such as gender, age and geographical location, if they wish, but they are not obliged to do so, and even if they do, only other members can read these pages. In most cases, then, the only information available about users is contained in what they post to threads. As I will note in Chapters 5 and 6, this has implications for my analysis of Mumsnet Talk, as details of individual users' circumstances that might affect the interpretation of their words are often not known.

Each post to a Mumsnet Talk thread may be conceptualized, in conversational terms, as a single 'turn', because it cannot be disrupted part way through (Herring and Androutsopoulos 2015), although individual posts may contain multiple moves, such as replies to two or more previous messages (Androutsopoulos, 2006). There is usually a time delay between turns, because members read and contribute at their leisure, tending to dip in and out of a thread over a period of several hours, days, weeks or even longer, and different people may join the conversation at different times. Discussions within a thread therefore do not tend to take place in 'real time'. As with the quasi-synchronous interactions of internet relay chat, a thread may contain multiple separate streams of conversation, as contributors are able to easily access and respond to *all* posts from the larger thread at any time (Garcia and Jacobs, 1999). This asynchronicity means that adjacent turns may well be unrelated, and potentially seem to lack coherency, particularly to an outsider. However, this disrupted adjacency rarely causes problems for participants themselves, whose understanding of the interactional norms of the forum will usually enable them to 'reconstruct' the relationship between turns with relative ease (Herring and Androutsopoulos 2015).

As well as the disrupted adjacency of its asynchronous interactions, Mumsnet Talk may be relatively inaccessible to outsiders because of its users' language practices. Many of these practices are common to other digital contexts, but taken together, they constitute quite a distinctive set of resources that contribute to the formation of in-group interactional norms. For example, contributors frequently use distinctive acronyms, such as MN (Mumsnet), DC (darling child) and PFB (precious first-born). Mumsnet acronyms can be particularly idiosyncratic, making it difficult for outsiders to decode many posts to the forum. Members will understand that the acronym 'AIBU' (am I being unreasonable?), for instance, is representative

of an entire sub-group of threads with a distinctive style, in which the instigator of the thread invites others' perspectives on a personal grievance or
complaint. There are also a range of other terms and phrases that demand
in-group knowledge, such as the euphemism 'she who must not be named',
which refers to the childcare expert and author Gina Ford, with whom Mumsnet had a legal dispute between 2006 and 2007, and specialist terms, such
as 'attachment parent' (which is explained in Chapter 6). Mumsnet users
also make creative and playful use of keyboard functions. For example,
they often employ a range of graphological forms to create different meanings and effects, as illustrated in Table 3.1. The use of strikethrough text
is a particularly interesting example of such keyboard creativity: as with

Table 3.1 Some graphological forms commonly used in Mumsnet Talk

Resource	*Examples*	*Explanation*
Strikethrough text	'little ~~cow~~ darling'; 'don't fight it ~~or are you shallow~~'	A line is placed through the text but the text remains visible – often used to imply awareness that what is written is taboo, offensive or a slip of the tongue
Asterisks	*voice; explana*tory*	Used for a range of functions, including corrections and emphasis
Brackets	\<sideways look and inward tut tut\>; \<\<shrugs\>\>; {preens}; (whispers); \<\<and we have a winner\>\>	Can represent non-verbal actions, sounds, directions or 'off-stage' announcements
Sounds presented in written form	'bleeugh'; 'Pahaha. He sounds so funny'.	Sounds, often expressive or emphatic, presented in approximated written form
Capitals	'I am right, I AM!'	Usually used for emphasis, to imply loud volume
Emojis and images	😃 🙂 😆 📗 🎉	Contributors can insert emojis and images in their posts, selecting from a limited range available within the platform
Unconventional punctuation and spelling	'these threads are. . . . . booooooooooooring'; 'you clean your loo brush in the dishwasher?!?!?!?!?!'	Used for a range of functions – for example to express timing, emphasis or surprise

acronyms, it can be used to signal meanings that only 'insiders' can understand. For example, in one post to a Mumsnet Talk thread titled 'Can we have a child exchange?' (which is introduced fully in Chapter 4), WhispersofWickedness uses both strikethrough text and acronyms in the following evaluative description of her son: 'I have a ~~PITA~~ cheeky 4 yo who NEEDS to go to school now'. Here, WhispersofWickedness's use of the acronym PITA (pain in the arse) obscures the meaning of this negative evaluation for 'outsiders' who may not be familiar with this acronym, whilst at the same time drawing on the shared understanding and experiences of her fellow Mumsnet users, who are likely both to know what PITA means and to have experienced similar frustrations with their own children. Such invocations of shared knowledge, resources and experiences contribute to a sense that Mumsnet is a community where individuals can come together and interact with others who have shared interests and values, and in which its users feel a sense of affiliation with one another. This insight, and some of its wider implications, is further explored in Chapter 6.

Studies of parenting forums around the world, such as Hong Kong's 'Happy Land' (Chan, 2008), Sweden's 'Familjeliv' (Hanell and Salö, 2017) and Canada's 'Momstown' (Mulcahy, Parry and Glover, 2015), as well as similar sites in Ireland (Brady and Guerin, 2010) and the US (Moravec, 2011), have suggested that forums comparable to Mumsnet have a similar ethos. These studies testify to the importance of online parenting forums in the lives of many parents, suggesting that they can offer safe, supportive environments in which mothers can be themselves, express their views honestly and value their shared expertise above that of medical or other experts. Such studies have also suggested that women's interactions in online parenting forums may work to shift and challenge dominant forms of knowledge around femininity, pregnancy and motherhood. Previous studies of Mumsnet Talk, for example, have shown that users of this forum frequently disrupt the stereotype that women's interactions will be polite and supportive, through their use of language and interactional styles that have been associated with hegemonic masculinity, such as swearing and confrontational debate (Pedersen and Smithson, 2013). Further, Pedersen (2016) has suggested that Mumsnet Talk users challenge ideals of 'good motherhood' that revolve around the 'intensive mothering' model by reconceptualizing decisions that may be considered 'selfish' within this model, such as bottle feeding or working full-time, as beneficial for both mother and child. Jensen (2013: 142) has shown that Mumsnet Talk is a space in which members can engage in 'struggles over what constitutes good, better and best parenting practice', pointing to a thread in which Mumsnet users 'defensively ward off' caricatures of 'perfect mothers', including 'Mother Earth' and 'militant mums'. Similarly, Jaworska (2017) shows that contributors to Mumsnet

Talk threads about postnatal depression are able to momentarily position themselves outside of the ideal of the 'good mother' by sharing confessional stories that disrupt the ideals associated with this subject position. She suggests that Mumsnet users' anonymity and the potential for immediate feedback from other contributors, which are features of most parenting forums, facilitate this kind of transformative process. She also shows that the flexibility of the discussion forum facilitates these negotiations, allowing Mumsnet users to take up a wide range of communicative resources, such as the narrative practices of *small confessions* and *exemplums*. Further evidence that Mumsnet Talk contributors employ a diverse range of communicative resources in this context is offered in Chapters 5 and 6.

As with explorations of gender and identity online, however, studies of online parenting forums have often shown that interactions within these spaces will rarely be exclusively transgressive in nature: rather, they are likely to draw on complex negotiations between individual autonomy, dominant discourses and local norms of sharing and interaction. For example, Madge and O'Connor (2006) point to the freedom, support and empowerment that the UK site babyworld, and others like it, offers its users. Yet they also show that 'traditional stereotypes of mothering and gender roles' prevail in contributors' self-introductions as the main carer, in a two-person heterosexual relationship (Madge and O'Connor, 2006: 56). A number of researchers have suggested that the consumerist element of many parenting sites works to perpetuate such restrictive norms. Jensen (2013), for example, argues that the way members are encouraged to interact with the Mumsnet website frames their interactions in this space within neoliberal discourses of choice, consumption and individualism. She points to the way that users are required, at the point of registration, to provide a number of personal details about themselves and their families, and invited to sign up to various emails and notifications, including those that offer reviews and discounts from a variety of businesses. Members can also, she notes, buy into the consumerist interests of the site by signing up to review products and services, and completing surveys and activities, in order to benefit third-party market research. In a North American context, both Worthington (2005) and Boon and Pentney (2015) emphasize the way that the corporate interests of the relatively large, public parenting sites iVillage and BabyCenter shape participation in these spaces, constraining individual users' autonomy and leading to the propagation of restrictive discourses of femininity and parenthood. Boon and Pentney (2015: 1763), for example, note that the architecture of BabyCenter, which tends to portray white, heterosexual couples and white babies in its fixed, edited and advertising images, 'influences who participates in and feels a part of the community'. It is therefore not surprising, they suggest, that breastfeeding selfies posted in this space conform to norms and expectations around femininity and the maternal body, reinforcing the 'status quo' through their exclusive reference to white, cisgender, heteronormative families that align with normative body ideals.

Such claims about the potential restrictions of online parenting sites echo the warnings of van Dijck (2013) and Thurlow (2013), who have cautioned against the premature celebration of the community-based internet over hierarchical, corporate media. Van Dijck (2013) points to the increased control that major corporations have over the ways in which users interact within digital platforms, explaining that affordances are programmed into large, global social network sites like Facebook and Blogger with specific objectives in mind, and that these objectives are ultimately driven more by profit motives than user communities. These critiques are mainly directed towards major corporations, like Facebook, YouTube and Google, rather than organizations such as Mumsnet and iVillage, which appear relatively small by comparison. However, these parenting sites, and others like them, are nevertheless profit-making companies that rely heavily on advertising revenue: in this way they are by no means communal spaces that are run exclusively by and for their users, or that are free from corporate demands and constraints. The power of the corporation within platforms such as Facebook, YouTube and, of course, Mumsnet, however, should also not be *over*-emphasized. The companies controlling these sites are certainly able to 'direct human sociability' (van Dijck, 2013: 13). However, the affordances of these sites are not fixed; they are also shaped by their users, who appropriate and negotiate digital affordances to suit their needs.

It is apparent from the review and discussion presented so far that the relationship between those who create, control and fund parenting websites and the users of these sites is complex and multi-faceted. Users are not completely free to interact in any imaginable way within parenting discussion forums, but at the same time those who run and fund these sites do not have complete control over the interactions that unfold in these spaces. The affordances of parenting discussion forums such as Mumsnet Talk are perhaps best conceptualized, then, as mutually constituted and shaped between the platforms themselves and their users (van Dijck, 2013; also see Barton and Lee, 2013; Page, Barton, Unger and Zappavigna, 2014). Exploring what Mumsnet Talk can offer, and what is possible in this space, is therefore a matter of exploring what kind of space has been carved out by the creators *and* users of this site, drawing on the range of linguistic, digital and social resources that are available to them.

Concluding remarks

This chapter has considered the question of whether internet discussion forums such as Mumsnet Talk, and other interactive digital contexts, can be fruitful sites for the negotiation, subversion and resistance of dominant cultural norms. A good deal of research has suggested that this may indeed be the case, and has emphasized the many possibilities that digital contexts may offer, including heightened freedom in terms of who individuals interact with, when and how, and what particular 'selves' they present to others. However, these findings are tempered by an acknowledgement of the socio-cultural constraints that remain across all modes of communication, and the particular structural and institutional constraints of relatively large websites such as Mumsnet Talk. Thus, whilst dominant norms, identities and stereotypes can be challenged through digital interactions, potentially making way for diverse and transformative forms of self-expression and identity, it is equally likely that these norms will prevail, as they often do in a wider social context.

In response to the insights that are offered by research exploring gender, parenthood and identity online, this book considers not only how Mumsnet Talk users may negotiate new ways of being a woman, parent or mother but also whether this context may engender constraints that actually work to *restrict* users' access to multiple and diverse subject positions. It differs from previous literature, however, because it pays much closer attention to the nature of the social forces – the *discourses* – that are at work in Mumsnet users' digital interactions. Further, it will explore *how* discourses of gender and parenthood are played out in Mumsnet Talk, through close linguistic scrutiny of the specific resources, affordances and possibilities that are deployed in these interactions. The nature of this approach to the exploration of language, gender and parenthood in Mumsnet Talk will be explored in the chapter that follows. This chapter will also emphasize the value of a self-reflexive stance, showing how a recognition of my own voice and values influenced the design, development and analysis of the Mumsnet study.

4   Researching Mumsnet Talk

The central challenge of this book lies in unpacking the ways in which Mumsnet Talk users communicate (either directly or indirectly) about parenting, motherhood and identity, and then piecing these fragments back together again. By doing so, I hope to draw out coherent insights about what discourses are at play in Mumsnet Talk, and what this can tell us about how parenting and motherhood can be navigated online. Finding ways of identifying and analyzing discourses in order to reveal these kinds of insights is also a challenge for the social sciences more widely. In Chapter 2, I pointed out that previous discursive studies of parenting and motherhood in a range of contexts have tended not to rise to this challenge. Such studies have often neglected, first, the central role that language plays in discursive struggles, and second, any clear explication of the means by which they arrive at claims about the presence of discourses. Even within the disciplines of sociolinguistics and discourse studies, which are well placed to advance linguistic methods for identifying and analyzing discourses, there has still been relatively little in the way of methodological insights, although there are notable exceptions in the work of analysts such as Baxter (2003), Reisigl and Wodak (2009) and Sunderland (2000, 2004).

This chapter offers a methodological contribution to discourse studies, including digital discourse studies, by providing a clear and detailed explanation of the methods of discourse identification and analysis that were employed in the Mumsnet study. Outlining this approach is valuable for discourse studies scholars because it shows, first, how a number of influences – namely feminist poststructuralist theory, the qualitative traditions of ethnography and grounded theory, and linguistic discourse analysis – can be productively brought together to identify and analyze discourses in a transparent and systematic way. Second, I show how researchers of digital contexts, who may not have the same opportunities for self-reflection as researchers who meet their participants in person, can nevertheless position themselves within the research site, and scrutinize their own role in the research process. I do so by explaining how I negotiated a self-reflexive stance as an 'observer-participant' throughout the Mumsnet study, and how this stance enhanced the research and analytical process.

The Mumsnet study: a qualitative, poststructuralist framework

The Mumsnet study is situated within a tradition of qualitative research, which tends to be small-scale, employs inductive logic, values the research-er's subjectivity and presents findings in a descriptive, non-numerical way (Robson, 2011). In keeping with the qualitative paradigm, it is structured in a flexible and emergent way. This research therefore does not begin with a preconceived hypothesis or a rigid methodological structure, but with a relatively open research question, namely 'how do Mumsnet users negotiate norms of gender, parenting and motherhood through their digi-tal interactions?', which is refined as the research progresses. The study's methodology, analysis and findings are emergent, being guided by its cen-tral aims, the data and iterative engagement with a range of literature. This can be described as a *pragmatic* research design, where the quest for a better understanding of the subject guides methodological choices (Den-zin and Lincoln, 2008; Dörnyei, 2007; Silverman, 2011). This qualitative, pragmatic approach is closely aligned with feminist poststructuralist theo-ries (as outlined in Chapter 2) because it facilitates flexibility and open-ness to multiple possibilities throughout the research process. It is able to support rich, in-depth explorations of *how* particular social situations are constructed (Denzin and Lincoln, 2008; J. Mason, 2002) – in this case, how users of Mumsnet Talk negotiate their parental identities in relation to wider discursive forces.

The inductive and iterative design of the Mumsnet study, which is cap-tured in diagrammatic form in Figure 4.1, takes particular inspiration from the established qualitative traditions of ethnography and grounded theory, in terms of both their shared principles and specific methods. Although it cannot be described as either a 'full' or 'traditional' grounded theory *or* ethnography, the foundational principles of flexibility, inductive analysis and emergent theory underpin its development. Both of these approaches emerged as a response to the positivist paradigm, which strives towards objectivity, generalizability and standardization, usually testing hypotheses through logic, employing prescriptive methods and proceeding in a pre-determined, linear fashion (Agar, 1995; Hammersley and Atkinson, 2007; Hine, 2000). These traditions offer an alternative, promoting the develop-ment of insights, analysis and theory directly from the research context and data in a non-linear way. By taking this approach, researchers are well

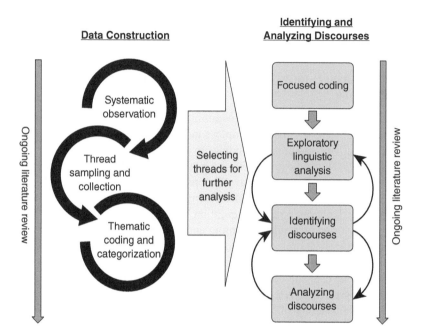

Figure 4.1 Research design

placed to engage with in-depth analyses, appreciate multiple perspectives and reach a point of deep understanding.

Neither ethnography nor grounded theory necessarily prescribes static, unified approaches. Ethnography, for example, is not allied to a particular method and generally does not proceed from a pre-determined research design (Hammersley and Atkinson, 2007; Hine, 2009). Ethnographic research is united, instead, by the goal of understanding cultures (Hine, 2000) and the principles of openness and flexibility. The ethnographic researcher traditionally enters the field of interest with an open mind and no fixed goal, and the research design becomes more refined as insights begin to emerge (Hammersley and Atkinson, 2007). Ethnographic methods have been utilized and adapted by a range of disciplines and for a range of social inquiries (Silverman, 2011), without necessarily making a commitment to the full immersion in a culture that is traditionally associated with ethnography (Green and Bloome, 1997). Like many other researchers of online communities and interactions (e.g. Androutsopoulos, 2008; Hine, 2000; Leppänen and Kytölä, 2017; Vaisman, 2013), I draw on ethnographic methods as they are relevant to my study and aims. For example, as I will explain in this chapter, I use a form of observation that is adapted from traditional face-to-face contact as a way into the Mumsnet Talk forum, a starting point for my analysis of interactions within this space.

As with ethnographic approaches, methods associated with grounded theory have frequently been adapted and adjusted in recent years. Although Glaser and Strauss's (1967) original realization of grounded theory remained committed to positivist principles, such as procedural rigour, prescriptive techniques and objectivity, the work of what Birks and Mills (2011: 3) call a 'second generation' of theorists, such as Clarke (2003) and Charmaz (2008, 2014), has resisted mechanical applications of grounded theory methods, pointing out that many researchers have successfully emphasized different criteria for grounded theory research, and that grounded theory techniques can be adopted without full commitment to its traditional procedural rigour. The approach taken in the Mumsnet study is aligned with this second generation, particularly Charmaz's (2014) 'constructivist grounded theory', which is broadly consistent with the poststructuralist outlook outlined in Chapter 2. The core principles of inductive logic and rigorous comparative and theoretical analysis that underpin this iteration of grounded theory (Charmaz, 2014) are central to the Mumsnet study. Grounded theory principles and procedures are particularly relevant during the first stage of this study, 'data construction', where I adopt methods such as memo writing and coding to facilitate my early familiarization with, and analysis of, Mumsnet Talk threads.

Being able to acknowledge one's own position within the research process is an important part of qualitative research that is foregrounded within both ethnography and constructivist grounded theory. A self-reflexive stance is also consistent with the poststructuralist perspective that 'truth', 'knowledge' and the research process itself are constructions, which reflect the researcher's background, values and interpretation of the data, rather than capturing an 'empirical reality' (Charmaz, 2014: 155). The Mumsnet study is supported by a self-reflexive stance throughout, whereby I acknowledge and critically examine my own position as a researcher and the values and perspectives that I bring to this research. Further examples throughout this chapter show how reflecting on my own practices and positioning myself on equal terms with Mumsnet users has supported my identification of key moments of resistance against perceived norms in the Talk forum. I also show how a self-reflexive stance has influenced my approach to ethical considerations.

The Mumsnet study is organized in two broad stages: 'data construction' and 'identifying and analyzing discourses' (see Figure 4.1). The processes involved at each of these stages are examined in detail in the sections that follow.

Data construction

As well as research itself, the material on which research is based, usually called 'data', is conceptualized as a constructed phenomenon in this book. In other words, I see 'data' as artefacts that come to exist as such only because of the research process, and will likely be perceived in different ways, depending on how and why they are collected, collated and analyzed (Charmaz and Bryant, 2011; Dey, 1993; Markham, 2013). I therefore use the phrase 'data construction', rather than, for example, 'data collection', to describe the first stage of the Mumsnet study, where threads are taken from the Mumsnet Talk forum and constructed as data for research purposes.

The data construction stage of the Mumsnet study was a process of discovery and exploration, where I gained an in-depth understanding of Mumsnet Talk, my self-positioning as a researcher and key themes in selected threads from the forum. I drew on several specific methods associated with grounded theory and ethnography at this stage. For example, grounded theory methods such as memo writing and thematic coding, as well as ethnographic observation, facilitated my early familiarization with, and analysis of, Mumsnet Talk interactions. In line with the principles of grounded theory and ethnography, these processes advanced iteratively. A cycle of observation, thread collection, continual engagement with wider literature and coding took place over a period of five months, between April and September 2014. The key outcome of these processes was the construction of a corpus of 50 threads comprising a total of just under 220,000 words, and a set of categories that captured the key themes of these threads. This section details the processes by which these data were constructed.

Systematic observation, memo writing and data collection

Observations of the Mumsnet Talk forum provided a starting point for the inductive exploration of interactions within this space. The nature of these observations was adapted for a digital context where, rather than observing people in face-to-face settings, I was essentially observing the written interactions they had created (Markham, 2004). The term 'systematic observation' (Androutsopoulos, 2008) foregrounds this committed, focused exploration of the complex fabric of the research context at given moments, as I experienced them. It also backgrounds the notion of time, which is less relevant in 'chrono-malleable' (Markham, 2004: 103) digital contexts, such as Mumsnet Talk, where a 'conversation' can take place over several days, weeks or even months, yet remain focused and cohesive. The process of systematic observation involved visiting the Mumsnet Talk forum regularly (on average, one hour per weekday) and observing the discussions that were taking place. I usually observed current activity, clicking the 'active' thread hyperlink on entering the site, although my explorations sometimes led me to older, archived threads. As my observations progressed, I reflected on my own position in relation to the Talk forum and its contributors, in keeping with the self-reflexive stance that is so valuable for poststructuralist and qualitative research (see earlier). At first, I saw myself as an outsider in the world of Mumsnet, and positioned myself very much as an observer. However, my stance as a researcher gradually shifted through the course of my observations.

I was not a member of Mumsnet before I began this research, and although I had often visited the site, I had never (and still have not) contributed to the forum. At the start of the research process, I therefore saw myself as a relative outsider in the world of Mumsnet, and positioned myself very much as an observer. However, as I engaged with the forum, I began to realize that, in many ways, I was a fairly typical Mumsnet user. Like many members of the site (see Chapter 1), I am white, British, well educated, middle class and a feminist. I have two children, am married to the father of these children, and we have a stable family life: we own our home, which our children have lived in all their lives, and both bring in a steady income. We have a parenting philosophy of sorts, and often spend time discussing how to approach the latest phase our children are going through. Finally, I regularly use digital media to connect with like-minded others, both personally and professionally. I also enjoy writing, and generally find it much easier to communicate my thoughts and feelings in written, as opposed to spoken, media. It is therefore not surprising that during my observations of Mumsnet Talk I have often read posts that express almost precisely my own thoughts on a subject, or which were written by an individual whose background and perspective appeared to be very similar to my own. For example, in one post I encountered early on in my research (and wrote about in a memo), a Mumsnet user revealed that she was an academic whose research was feminist in nature, and that she had found it difficult to balance her research with her everyday home life. I could have written the post myself.

I was able to capture some of the early responses and reflections that shaped my engagement with the Mumsnet Talk forum through memo writing, a process that can be likened to writing ethnographic field notes. I wrote memos throughout the data construction process to record my thoughts, reflections and developing interpretations and to justify my sampling decisions. In keeping with grounded theory traditions, my memos tended to be quite detailed and sometimes included analytical comments

(Corbin and Strauss, 2008). The process of memo writing was well suited to the digital research context because I was able to take 'time out' of my observations to write memos without leaving or disturbing the research setting. Equally, useful insights often surfaced later, after leaving the research site, and sometimes unexpectedly. Thus, my memo writing was dictated not by time or place but by emerging insights, whenever these occurred (see Charmaz, 2014). For example, a couple of weeks after reading a Mumsnet thread about 'forgetting children', a personal experience led me to re-evaluate my initial reactions to this thread. I captured this shift in perspective by writing a memo, part of which is reproduced in Extract 4.1.

Extract 4.1 Excerpt from a memo written after revisiting a thread about 'forgetting children', 14.05.2014

My initial reaction was that this [forgetting your child] was a horrible thing to 'show off' about and made me consider whether a criticism I'd read of Mumsnet, that mothers compete as to who can be the worst mother, was perhaps relevant here. A week or so later my own daughter was left at nursery because of a mix-up with the childminder. I felt guilty and upset about this, and remembered another occasion when my husband had forgotten to collect both of our children from nursery. Again, I had felt incredibly guilty and upset, and worried that my older son, in particular, might somehow lose trust in us or be 'damaged' in the long term because of this mistake. I thought again of this thread but with a different perspective. I felt ashamed about my initial reaction that forgetting a child was an awful thing to do, and perhaps shouldn't be shared with others.

By writing memos, I was able to examine my role as a 'constructor' of data (J. Mason, 2002: 99) and reflect on factors that might have influenced my feelings towards and interpretations of data. To offer another example, my initial response to a thread titled 'Your identity as a mother', recorded in the memo sampled in Extract 4.2, reveals my personal resistance to being identified as a 'mum', despite the fact that I frequently identify myself in this way in my own written and spoken interactions. Writing this memo encouraged me to acknowledge and interrogate my negative feelings towards being identified as a 'mum' and, later, to recognize the transformative potential of subject positions such as 'parent', and the inclusion of fathers in women's writing about their family lives (see Chapter 2). This example again shows that the process of memo writing often supported my self-reflexive approach, providing opportunities to bring myself into the analysis of Mumsnet Talk threads.

Extract 4.2 Excerpt from a memo written in response to first reading the thread 'Your identity as a mother', 05.06.2014

Some cling to 'the real me' identity very fiercely, rejecting the 'mum' identity. I felt I could really identify with this, and sometimes felt that I reacted negatively to posters who very much identified as 'mums'.

Connecting with my personal responses to threads and individual posts led me to position myself on an equal footing with Mumsnet users, as well in the more unequal role of 'researcher' to my research 'subjects'. By situating myself within the research site, I was better able to understand it as a participant in this context. I therefore came, over time, to position myself as an *observer-participant* (J. Mason, 2002; see also Gold, 1958). This intermediary position between complete participant and complete observer foregrounds the researcher's observational role, which is appropriate here because I do not participate in interactions and users were not, at the time, aware of my presence. Yet it also allows me to acknowledge the participatory aspect of my role, including my personal engagement with the themes of the forum and my perceived affinity with Mumsnet users.

Through my observations of Mumsnet Talk interactions, and self-positioning as an 'observer-participant', I was able to gain insights into the benefits of being a member of Mumsnet and contributing to the Talk forum. For example, I discovered that many contributors receive both practical and emotional support in this space, which, though ostensibly 'public', provides resources for anonymity and facilitates quite personal, intimate interactions (these resources are outlined in more detail in Mackenzie, 2017b). I also found that many Mumsnet users feel a strong sense of belonging within this space (see Chapter 3). Such insights have allowed me to situate my detailed analysis of specific moments of interaction within the wider context of Mumsnet Talk. They have also had significant implications for the ethical decision-making process, which is explored in more detail towards the end of this chapter.

The process of systematic observation also, and importantly, facilitated the construction of a corpus of threads from the Mumsnet Talk forum. Through the course of my observations, threads were chosen through purposive sampling, whereby the aims of the study guided my selection of threads for further analysis (Robson, 2011). My criteria for the purposive selection of threads were based on my primary research question, which evolved over time (see earlier), but during the early stages of my study, read thus: 'How do Mumsnet users negotiate norms of *gender, parenting* and *motherhood* through their digital interactions?'

I kept this question close to hand throughout the process of data construction, and focused on the words highlighted in italics. These key terms offered flexible guidelines for data sampling. The words 'parenting' and 'motherhood', for example, prompted me to pay particular attention to threads with titles that included naming devices associated with the family, such as 'mother' and its variants, but also categories such as 'parent', 'father', 'husband', 'wife' and 'child', and their variants. The key term 'gender' encouraged me to look closely at threads with titles that seemed to make gender relevant. Any thread title using gendered familial categories, such as 'mother' or 'father' (or their variants) does this; the thread titles 'Your identity as a mother' and 'Your only purpose as a woman is to give birth' meet all three criteria. In addition, some threads were of potential interest even though their titles did not directly employ any of the categories outlined earlier. Often, during the observation and sampling processes, which were closely related, my attention wandered to threads that I found to be of personal interest, without any real consideration of whether they related to my primary research question. At such moments, my position as both an observer and a participant became particularly apparent. This strategy of making focused selections of threads combined with what might be described as interest-driven engagement with the site was a useful way of both gaining an in-depth understanding of the nature of interactions within the Talk forum and identifying threads of interest in relation to my aims and research questions. Extracts 4.3 and 4.4, which are taken from memos written during the process of observation and sampling, show how I applied these flexible sampling strategies in practice.

Extract 4.3 Excerpt from a memo written on 19.05.2014,
after selecting a thread titled 'DS keeps calling me Mum but
I want to be Mummy'

I chose this thread, as with so many others, both because it struck a personal chord and because I thought it might have some interesting discussion on what it means to be a 'mum'/'mummy'. On a personal note, I also have a strong desire to be called 'mummy' by my two children, and had never really considered why. They have both called me various other things but I also prefer 'mummy'. 'Mummy' struck me as quite a feminine term and I wondered if this contributed to my own and others' preference for it.

Extract 4.4 Excerpt from a memo written on 15.08.2014,
after selecting a thread titled 'Considering another baby and
thinking of DH taking "mat leave" instead of me'

I was immediately drawn to this thread because, on a personal level, I think it's fantastic that parents now have the option to do this, and I've often thought that my husband and I might do this if we had another child. I also thought this thread may offer 'alternative' perspectives on bringing up children that might contest existing 'norms' and that contributors may question the gendered division of parenting roles.

As I collected threads from the Mumsnet Talk forum, I began to re-read and code them, a process that is explained in more detail in the following subsection. The iterative process of observing, collecting and coding Mumsnet Talk threads meant that I was able to use my emerging understanding of key themes across the threads to inform subsequent data sampling. As I collected more threads, I began to seek out examples that offered new or different perspectives and would enrich my growing corpus rather than replicate the content I already had. Thus, I also drew on theoretical sampling methods, which 'focu[s] on finding *new data sources* . . . that can best explicitly address specific theoretically interesting facets of the emergent analysis' (Clarke, 2003: 577, her emphasis).

Thematic coding and categorization

Coding has been described by many grounded theorists as a process that fractures the data, before bringing it back together in new and meaningful ways (Charmaz, 2014; Glaser and Strauss, 1967; Strauss and Corbin, 1998). In the Mumsnet study, the coding process involved assigning descriptive labels, or 'codes', to stretches of text within threads, which usually led to the recognition of patterns and themes as more and more text was coded. Extract 4.5 provides an example of a code created at the data construction stage, and some of the excerpts from different threads that are captured within it. Coding took place in three stages: initial, axial and focused coding, which straddled the two stages of this study. In this section, I explain the nature of the initial and axial coding at the heart of the first (data construction) stage. The process of focused coding, which is part of the second stage, is detailed in the section that follows.

Extract 4.5 Excerpts from the code being a 'good mum'

1. Can you guess some have been a PITA [pain in the arse] already lecturing me (good mums don't, apparently, wear make-up: that money/time could be spent on PFB [precious first-born]).

2. our modern self-definition of motherhood 'I am a sensible empow-
ered woman – based on ME not just biology – who organizes/cares/
makes choices/reads up about parenting and am doing a great job
raising well balanced kids'
3. She is a wonderful mum and loves her DC [darling children] to
death

The 'initial' coding process (Charmaz, 2014) involved close, line-by-line
reading of sampled threads and the creation of codes to capture patterns or
emerging themes across and within these threads. At this juncture, multiple
passages of text from different threads were assigned to single codes, and
sometimes multiple codes to a single passage. Initial coding began without
any *a priori* codes or categories, so as not to restrict my reading of the
threads (Bazeley, 2007), or 'impose a framework' on my analysis (Charmaz,
2014: 150). The aims of the study, however, did have a significant influence
on this early coding. For example, several of the codes I created after reading the first ten threads, such as 'gender relevance' and 'constructions of
mother and motherhood', were closely related my initial research question.

This coding process was again consistent with an emergent and inductive
research design. As more threads were collected, read and coded, new codes
were created and existing codes were modified, refined and adjusted. For
example, as some early codes, such as 'constructions of mother and motherhood', became overloaded, I developed new codes that captured more
specific themes, such as:

- mothers act intuitively;
- mothers want to look after, care for and protect their children;
- fathers are forgetful and incompetent;
- mothers are guided by experts;
- mothers are associated with 'feminine' qualities and language;
- mothers are slim, healthy and attractive.

The construction of these codes was undoubtedly influenced by my personal
experiences, feminist perspective, and wider reading and scholarship in the
area of gender and motherhood. For example, engaging with a good deal of
critique around essentialist notions of gender and motherhood, particularly
the concept that women are 'naturally' predisposed to caring roles, made me
particularly alert to moments at which contributors alluded to their maternal
'intuitions', which were initially coded to 'mothers act intuitively'. However, all codes were subject to a rigorous process of continual self-reflective
critique, revision, adjustment, restructuring and renaming. For example, as
the coding process developed, I often found that Mumsnet users' own words

captured a concept in more succinct and compelling terms than mine. On such occasions, I created 'in vivo' code titles: labels taken directly from the words of participants, such as 'don't beat yourself up' and 'your only purpose as a woman is to give birth'. Creating in vivo codes allowed my participants' voices to be heard alongside my own, thus anchoring the analysis in my participants' worlds (Charmaz, 2014).

The shift towards using in vivo titles as the coding process developed was intertwined with a developing recognition of my own affinity and alignment with Mumsnet users, and the importance of valuing their voices in this study. The most significant change to my naming of codes, however, was a shift from identifying themes or 'types' of people to identifying actions and processes. For example, many initial code titles, such as 'mothers are slim, healthy and attractive' and the other examples offered earlier, persistently labelled parents, casting them, as Charmaz (2014) suggests this style of coding will do, with static labels. These titles also tended to be gendered, often naming mothers specifically, when in fact there were references to fathers in the threads that could be incorporated within the same codes. Reflecting on these labels led me to realize my own habit of generalizing by gender. I therefore began, as coding progressed, to move away from code titles such as 'mothers are. . .', 'mothers want. . .', and so on, which made universal assertions from isolated references, to titles that coded actions and processes. Table 4.1 illustrates this point by juxtaposing some initial and revised codes.

As well as refining the structure of individual codes and their references, I also began to organize codes in terms of hierarchies and relationships as this process developed, through what Strauss and Corbin (1998: 123) call 'axial coding'. This involved moving from a long list of 'free', unconnected codes to a 'tree' system (Gibbs, 2002; Bazeley, 2007). Within this system, broader superordinate categories encapsulated a number of more specific sub-categories as shown in Figure 4.2. Figure 4.3 displays all the categories created through the data construction process.

Table 4.1 A comparison of initial and revised codes

Initial codes	Revised codes
Mothers act intuitively	Acting intuitively
Mothers are creative	Being creative
Fathers are forgetful and incompetent	Forgetting your children
Mothers are guided by experts	Valuing expert advice
Mothers are calm, in control and responsible	Being calm, in control and responsible
Mothers are slim, healthy and attractive	Wanting to be slim, healthy and attractive

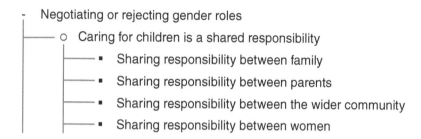

- Negotiating or rejecting gender roles
  - o Caring for children is a shared responsibility
    - ▪ Sharing responsibility between family
    - ▪ Sharing responsibility between parents
    - ▪ Sharing responsibility between the wider community
    - ▪ Sharing responsibility between women

Figure 4.2 Code tree for the category 'negotiating or rejecting gender roles'

- Constructing identities (sources 41; references 556)
- Describing or enacting gender roles (sources 49; references 1368)
- Describing or enacting parenting 'norms' (sources 49; references 1833)
- Factors influencing parenting 'norms' (sources 31; references 382)
- Negotiating or rejecting gender roles (sources 48; references 908)
- Negotiating or rejecting parenting 'norms' (sources 43; references 1008)

Figure 4.3 Final list of categories created at the data construction stage

Initial coding and axial coding were central to the data construction process and informed the progress of the Mumsnet study as a whole. These processes also supported the development of my critical and self-reflexive stance, by drawing attention to the views, values and assumptions I was bringing to my reading and analysis of Mumsnet Talk threads. For example, the coding process led me to recognize that I often *imposed* gender on my reading of threads at an early stage, as shown earlier. By acknowledging some of the ways in which I was 'constructing' this data as a coherent set of codes and categories, I was able to scrutinize my own role in the research process.

There are a number of qualitative data analysis (QDA) software packages that can support the kind of collection, coding and categorization of data that has been outlined earlier, such as Gephi, ATLAS.ti and MAX-QDA. QSR International's NVivo 10 (2012), however, was identified as the software best suited to the needs of this study. This program allows the researcher to create a project space and to collect and upload online data using the 'NCapture' function, which preserves internet pages in their original format. Coding is a key function of most QDA software, and within NVivo, coded text is stored and organized in nodes, which function as digital holding points for coded passages of text. Nodes can be either free, operating as separate entities, or organized in hierarchical relationships, so that related nodes can be grouped together within larger categories, coming to resemble a 'tree' structure, as shown in Figure 4.2. I also uploaded memos to the NVivo project space and linked these with the threads or nodes to which they related. Using QDA software to code and organize data supported the flexibility of this process, making it possible to edit and re-work codes, assign passages of text to multiple codes, and use searches to ask questions of the data, as I will explain in the section that follows.

The process of data construction came to a close at the point of 'saturation', where I felt that further observation, data collection or analysis would not 'shed . . . further light on the issue under investigation' (M. Mason, 2010: n.p.; also see Charmaz, 2014; Corbin and Strauss, 2008). Limiting the data construction process also involved practical considerations. For example, I allowed a maximum of six months for the whole process, because a significantly shorter allocation may not have generated the required data or depth of understanding, and a significantly longer allocation may have resulted in the generation of too much data, and/or delayed the progress of the study.

Selecting threads for further analysis

At the end of the first stage of the Mumsnet study, I had a corpus of 50 threads that made the themes of gender and/or parenthood relevant to interactions, either explicitly or implicitly. Through the data construction process, I gained not only an in-depth understanding of key themes in these threads but also a better appreciation of the nature of the Mumsnet Talk forum, the way members interacted within it, and my self-positioning as a researcher. However, in order to move forward with the study, I wanted to identify a smaller number of threads, so that I could conduct a more detailed, qualitative analysis that would facilitate my theorization about the specific discourses at play in Mumsnet Talk interactions, and allow me to draw out the multiple ways in which Mumsnet users could negotiate and position themselves in relation to these discourses.

In order to identify a smaller number of threads for close analysis, I focused on points at which different codes seemed to merge, interrelate or compete by using NVivo 10 to conduct matrix coding queries, which essentially checked for points of overlap between codes. For example, a matrix coding query revealed that a number of references from the 'enacting stereotypically "feminine" qualities and language' code were also coded to the following:

- sharing responsibility between the wider community (12 references from a possible 26);
- 'I love my children' (20 references from a possible 55);

- being positive about . . . your children (45 references from a possible 150);
- 'your only purpose as a woman is to give birth' (26 references from a possible 143);
- being negative about your children (24 references from a possible 131), and
- identifying as a mum (37 references from a possible 237).

. . . and that references from the 'using gender-neutral terminology' code were also coded to:

- identifying as a parent (27 references from a possible 246);
- 'I'm not just a mother' (12 references from a possible 141);
- mother as main parent (15 references from a possible 246);
- being in a heterosexual relationship (25 references from a possible 443);
- caring for children is a shared responsibility (19 references from a possible 410), and
- looking after mothers' needs (9 references from a possible 313).

These queries brought my attention to threads where Mumsnet users seemed to explore and negotiate different forms of knowledge and subjectivity in relation to the central concepts of gender and parenthood. This exploration of key codes and categories led to the identification of the threads 'Your identity as a mother' and 'Can we have a child exchange?' as particularly fruitful sites for further analysis.

In the 'Your identity as a mother' thread, the first contributor invites others to explore their 'experiences' of motherhood – in particular, how motherhood 'changes' them, and 'their view of themselves' (Extract 4.6). Contributors' quite explicit focus on identity and motherhood in this thread provided an opportunity to explore Mumsnet users' conscious self-positioning as 'mothers' (or more commonly, 'mums'), or their resistance of this subject position, and the meta-language surrounding 'motherhood' and 'identity'.

Extract 4.6 Opening post from 'Your identity as a mother'[1]

pandarific Sun 01-Jun-14 14:43:17

1. I've been reading a lot of fiction that deals with motherhood and
2. family relationships and I'm curious as to how it changes people,
3. and their view of themselves. Has your perception of who you
4. are changed since you had children? How much of your identity
5. is bound up with being a mum? Do you think the strength of
6. your desire to be a mum/what stage in your life you had them

7. affected the degree of the changes?

8. For some reason this has come out reading like an exam question
9. – it's not meant to be! Just curious about people's experiences.

The title and opening post of 'Can we have a child exchange?' (Extract 4.7) also introduce the thread's main premise, a mock exchange of children.

Extract 4.7 Opening post from 'Can we have a child exchange?'

BertieBotts Wed 16-Jul-14 13:23:30

1. I can offer one (currently) sweaty and exuberant 5 year old.
2. Reads most things. Speaks some German. Quite helpful around
3. the house.

4. Reason for sale: Excessive farting.

5. Any takers? 😁

Where 'Your identity as a mother' includes quite an earnest discussion about participants' identities, 'Can we have a child exchange?' is made up of largely playful, light-hearted, witty exchanges. Analyzing this thread therefore provided an opportunity to explore what participants' language choices might reveal about their self-positioning as 'mothers' (or indeed as something else) when they were *not* explicitly attending to their sense of self. Analyzing two such different interactional moments from Mumsnet Talk supported my overall aim of exploring the discourses and related subject positions that were available to and negotiated by Mumsnet users, providing more space for diversity within quite a focused, qualitative context.

Identifying and analyzing discourses

The first stage of the Mumsnet study, data construction, acted as a springboard for the second stage, identifying and analyzing discourses. As noted earlier, the aim of this second stage was to identify specific discourses in Mumsnet Talk interactions, and to explore the ways in which Mumsnet users negotiated and positioned themselves in relation to these discourses. In order to achieve this aim, I focused on just two threads from the larger corpus of 50: 'Your identity as a mother' and 'Can we have a child exchange?'. The process of thematic coding informed both the selection and initial analysis of these threads, and the principles of flexibility and emergent theory remained central to the concurrent identification and analysis of discourses at work in the interactions. However, as the second stage developed, I moved away from the analytical tools of grounded theory, and towards a qualitative linguistic analysis rooted in feminist poststructuralist theory. In this section, I detail the processes involved in this second part of the Mumsnet study: focused coding, exploratory linguistic analysis, and identifying and analyzing discourses.

Focused coding

After selecting two threads for further analysis, I coded these threads afresh and in more detail, this time paying attention to recurring linguistic structures as well as content themes. This focused coding process, which can be described as an accelerated version of initial and axial coding, was an important starting point in the process of identifying the discourses at work in Mumsnet Talk threads. Through focused coding, I began to theorize about larger structures at work in the selected threads, distinguishing a category of 'theoretical codes' that were indicative of discursive formations because they captured particular forms of knowledge, power and subjectivity. I also paid attention to peripheral codes and absences in the threads, in order to highlight what was *not said*, or was marginalized, in line with both Sunderland's (2000) and van Leeuwen's (1995, 1996) work on absences (see discussion in Chapter 2). For example, the 'references to men' code actually captures a *lack* of reference to men within 'Your identity as a mother', showing that mentions of men were marked in this thread and that they were unusual and worthy of special attention (I did not create a 'references to women' code; it would have very quickly become overloaded).

Focused coding of 'Your identity as a mother' and 'Can we have a child exchange?' led to the identification of the following theoretical codes.

'Your identity as a mother' theoretical codes:

- total motherhood;
- child-centricity;
- individuality;
- reference to men, and
- equality between parents.

'Can we have a child exchange?' theoretical codes:

- the classified advertisement frame;
- indexing gender;
- indexing class, and
- child-centricity.

These sets of theoretical codes began to reveal, in each case, an 'analytic story' (Charmaz, 2014) to be explored through further qualitative analysis. For example, the theoretical codes relating to 'Can we have a child exchange?' captured the way that contributors to this thread drew on distinctive sets of resources that brought to mind, in the first instance, the genre of classified advertisements, and in the second instance, cultural norms, expectations or stereotypes around gender and class. The ways in which I developed these analyses are further explored in the following sections.

Exploratory linguistic analysis

The focused coding of 'Your identity as a mother' and 'Can we have a child exchange?' created a 'skeleton' (Charmaz, 2014: 141) for the close linguistic analysis of these threads: a point from which I was able to move forward and add flesh to the analytical bones I had constructed. This linguistic analysis began by tracking references from the theoretical codes through each selected thread in turn, focusing on the linguistic features of each group of references. In line with a grounded, inductive approach, this analysis was relatively free and unstructured; I did not set out to investigate pre-established linguistic features, but to discover which features emerged in relation to particular forms of knowledge and subjectivity. Through this analytical process, I was able to further theorize about wider structures and identify potential discourses at work in the threads. The process of tracking a theoretical code through a thread, in order to identify linguistic features of interest and theorize about potential discourses, is illustrated ahead with reference to the codes 'total motherhood' and 'child-centricity', which relate to the 'Your identity as a mother' thread.

The theoretical code 'total motherhood' includes references in which participants convey a sense that 'motherhood' has a significant effect upon their lives and the ways in which they position themselves. It includes the following sub-categories:

- being a mum;
- being an 'attachment parent';
- 'I don't know who I am';
- inevitability of motherhood, and
- mother as 'whole woman'.

Many of the sub-categories listed here relate to how individuals are positioned as subjects, which is apparent through the frequency of the pronoun 'I', the relational verb 'be' (realized here as 'being' and 'am') and the category 'mum' or 'mother'. For example, the sub-category 'being a mum' includes multiple references in which participants categorize themselves as 'mums'. These self-categorizations point to the presence of a discursive force that offers distinct and binary subject positions along gendered lines, as 'mothers' and 'fathers': a potential discourse of 'gendered parenthood'. Further, where participants qualify 'mum' with an intensifier, as in the example 'I was 100% mum' (post 11), they suggest that the subject position 'mum' has 'total' influence over their sense of self. This points to a potential discourse of 'total motherhood', which can also be subsumed within the overarching discourse of 'gendered parenthood'. The fact that a number of sub-categories within 'total motherhood' have competing counterparts within this thread also points to the discursive struggles that contributors engage with, in order to negotiate and define their own subjectivity. For example, 'being a mum' can be said to compete with the codes 'being me', 'being a parent' and 'being a worker, having a job or career'.

The theoretical code 'child-centricity' combines references in which participants use a range of linguistic and digital resources (e.g. the graphological forms outlined in Chapter 3) to express their positive feelings for and commitment to their children. It includes the following sub-categories:

- being 'needed' by children;
- expressing love for children;
- 'I don't matter';
- positivity towards children;
- pride in children, and
- putting children first.

As with 'total motherhood', several sub-categories of 'child-centricity' can be paired with 'competing' counterparts. For example, many references within the codes 'fake it till you make it' and 'cut yourself some slack' contrast with the expressions of love and selflessness within the codes 'expressing love for children' and 'putting children first'. These competing expressions again point to a struggle to define forms of knowledge and subjectivity surrounding children and Mumsnet users' relations to them.

Identifying and analyzing discourses

Following the focused coding and exploratory linguistic analyses of 'Your identity as a mother' and 'Can we have a child exchange?', I further developed my analysis and theorization about the discourses at work in these threads by exploring moments of convergence, interrelation and competition between potential discourses such as those mentioned earlier. In order to do this, I identified an interactional sequence of particular interest, a 'significant moment', from each thread. My first criterion for identifying these moments was that there must be some evidence of interaction between participants, whereby they respond to one another through direct address, by answering each other's questions, or by picking up on themes others have introduced. The second criterion differed for each thread. From 'Your identity as a mother', I identified a moment of discursive struggle (Baxter, 2003): a site of contested knowledge, power and subjectivity (see Chapter 2). In the 'Can we have a child exchange?' thread, however, no single sequence stood out as being more discursively 'significant' than others: posts to this thread are far more uniform in style and consistent in the way their authors draw on, and position themselves in relation to, a group of discourses. I therefore chose a sequence that I judged to be representative of the thread as a whole.

Davies and Harré's (1990) theory of positioning provided a useful framework for analyzing these significant moments with a focus on the discursive nexus of knowledge, power and subjectivity. For Davies and Harré (1990), it is through social interaction that individuals are positioned as subjects. These positions may be fleeting, or relatively stable, and individuals may be positioned in multiple or contradictory ways through the course of interaction, by drawing on a range of resources to discursively position themselves and others. Three linguistic resources for self-positioning emerged as particularly relevant in Mumsnet users' interactions: (1) indexing, (2) double-voicing and (3) evaluation. The concept of indexicality, and the way it is deployed in this study, is further explained at the start of Chapter 5. The relevance of double-voicing and evaluation is explored ahead, in a worked example that demonstrates how I explored and adjusted the boundaries of the potential discourses of 'gendered parenthood', 'total motherhood' and 'child-centricity' in my analysis of a post from the 'Your identity as a mother' thread.

In post 66 to 'Your identity as a mother' (Extract 4.8), the potential discourses of 'gendered parenthood', 'child-centricity' and 'total motherhood' seem to merge, as MrsPennyapple equates total devotion to her children with her role as a 'good mum' and conveys her exasperation with the sense that this role is all that matters in her life.

Extract 4.8 Excerpt from post 66 to 'Your identity as a mother'

MrsPennyapple Wed 04-Jun-14 12:04:45

1. At the moment I am filled with the overwhelming sense that I
2. just don't matter. It doesn't matter if I come on my period and am
3. bleeding heavily and just want to take two minutes in the
4. bathroom by myself. It doesn't matter if something I want to hear

5. has come on the news. It doesn't matter if I've had a shit night's
6. sleep. I have tried to talk to DH about it but he just doesn't get it.
7. Last night he responded with 'but you're a good mum, and that's
8. what's important'. Just completely compounded and confirmed
9. everything I'm feeling. I am the least important person in my
10. own life.

Through her repeated expressions of the notion that her own life does not 'matter' by comparison with her children's lives, MrsPennyapple positions herself as a 'child-centred', 'total mother': a subject who is entirely defined by her relation to her children. In this post, the potential discourses of 'child-centricity' and 'total motherhood' merge in such a way as to suggest that they may in fact come together as *one* discourse that positions women, as 'mothers', entirely in relation to children. I came to name this the 'child-centric motherhood' discourse.

The 'child-centric motherhood' discourse is perhaps expressed most clearly when MrsPennyapple reproduces the 'voice' of her husband, whose words (lines 7-8) position her as a 'good mum' and imply that being a good mum is the only important thing in her life. In this example, MrsPennyapple uses a strategy that has been widely recognized in sociolinguistic research on language, interaction and identity, which Baxter (2014) calls *double-voicing*. Reframing Bakhtin's (1984 [1963]) concept of double-voiced discourse for a linguistic context, Baxter (2014: 4) explains that double-voicing involves bringing together one individual's words, thoughts or intentions with those of another, so that in effect, two (or more) 'voices' can be represented within a single utterance. This contrasts with 'single-voicing', whereby 'the orientation of the speaker is principally to themselves and to perpetuating their own agenda, rather than to engaging with the interests and concerns of others' (Baxter, 2014: 4). Her analyses focus on the use of double-voicing to ward off a threat that is represented by another interlocutor (whether real or imagined) and she distinguishes five types: anticipatory, corrective, mitigating, authoritative and dialogic. MrsPennyapple's words are an example of 'dialogic double-voicing', a type that is particularly common in the threads analyzed here, whereby ideas are debated 'as if the speaker is both the addresser and the addressee' (Baxter, 2014: 5). Dialogic double-voicing usually involves an internal debate of two sides of an argument, and a personal defence against another's point of view. In this case, the point of view being contested is that being a 'good mum' is the most important thing in MrsPennyapple's life. This use of dialogic double-voicing distances her from the message that being a good mum is all that should matter to her, and by using it, she resists being positioned by the 'child-centric motherhood' discourse.

In MrsPennyapple's post, and elsewhere in 'Your identity as a mother', another key resource by which Mumsnet contributors work to position themselves and others is *evaluation*. In order to understand and interpret contributors' use of this resource from a poststructuralist perspective, I turned to the work of Du Bois (2007), whose 'stance triangle' (see Figure 4.4) focuses the analyst's attention on how individuals are intersubjectively positioned through evaluation; that is, how they are positioned through the way they relate to and align with others. This alignment may be positive, negative or at some point along a continuous scale between the two. MrsPennyapple's alignment with her husband is negative. This much is apparent through complaints such as 'I have tried to talk to DH' and 'he just doesn't get it' (line 6), which point to her perceived difficulty in communicating with her husband. Both the verb 'tried' and the intensifier 'just' convey her effort and exasperation at his lack of understanding. Her use of the same intensifier in line 8, together with the intensifying adverb 'completely', the verbs 'compounded and confirmed' and the rhetorical functions of alliteration and repetition in threes, further communicates a feeling of frustration and conflict with her husband. Through this negative alignment, MrsPennyapple further

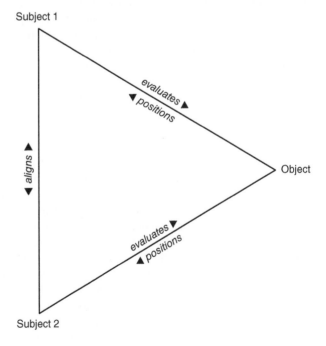

Figure 4.4 Du Bois's (2007: 163) 'stance triangle'

resists being positioned by the 'child-centric motherhood' discourse that her husband comes to represent within this post.

The worked example that has been presented in this section shows how a theoretical linguistic approach was realized in practice, through close attention to the ways in which forms of knowledge, power and subjectivity are constituted in the Mumsnet Talk threads. By identifying some of the specific linguistic mechanisms by which this central triad of discourse theory operates, I was able to identify the discourses that constitute particular norms and assumptions about gender and parenthood in Mumsnet users' interactions, and to explore the multiple ways in which Mumsnet users positioned themselves and others in relation to these discourses. The products of these analyses are detailed in the chapters that follow, beginning with an explication of the eight discourses that are identified through analysis of Mumsnet Talk interactions, in Chapter 5.

Ethical considerations

As detailed earlier, through the course of the Mumsnet study my stance shifted from that of a relatively detached observer to a more involved observer-participant. This shift, and my growing understanding of the Mumsnet Talk forum from the perspective of a participant, helped me to situate the detailed analysis of specific moments of interaction within the wider context of Mumsnet Talk. It also significantly affected the ethical decision-making processes involved in this study. This section details the ways in which it did so, and the decisions I ultimately took in order to minimize the potential for my research to cause harm of any kind.

My initial considerations of ethical issues were influenced by my perception of Mumsnet Talk as a 'public' forum: in other words, a forum that is readily accessible to anyone with an internet connection. Many internet researchers have suggested that where data are sourced from contexts like this, consent from participants is probably not necessary (Androutsopoulos, 2008; Sveningsson Elm, 2009; Thelwall and Wilkinson, 2010). This is based on the assumption that users of 'public' spaces have waived their rights to privacy, confidentiality and autonomy, and thus it is not unfair or harmful to access and use this information for research purposes. However, my engagement and affiliation with the Mumsnet Talk forum and its users led me to take a more case-based, context-sensitive approach (Mackenzie, 2017b; Markham and Buchanan, 2012, 2015; Spilioti, 2017), and subsequently, to recognize certain norms of interaction and information sharing within this online space that were at odds with my early views. For example, I felt that many contributors addressed quite a specific audience that did not include me (as a researcher, at least). Indeed, I thought it very unlikely that many users would expect a researcher to take an interest in their contributions to this busy forum. In addition, it became clear that a lot of Mumsnet users placed high value on their sense of privacy and anonymity, with many exercising their autonomy and agency in imaginative ways, in order to control and shape the accessibility of their posts and the degree to which they could be identified as individual users (the ways in which they do so are further explored in Mackenzie, 2017b).

By acknowledging my own engagement with and position within the Talk forum, I was able to recognize the potential for my research to cause harm through violating norms of information sharing within Mumsnet Talk, and to re-evaluate my research decisions accordingly. One of the most significant changes I made as a result of these considerations was to contact all of the Mumsnet users whose words I wished to quote and/or analyze in detail, to ask for their informed consent, and give them the option to (1) have their usernames anonymized, and (2) to withdraw at any time. It is worth noting, however, that there are many other researchers who have not sought consent from individual contributors to use similar publicly accessible discussion forum posts, and that seeking consent may not be deemed appropriate by all researchers of online forums in all circumstances. For example, in Jaworska's (2017) study of 18 discussions about post-natal depression on Mumsnet Talk, she does not seek consent from contributors to these threads on the grounds that these data have not been directly elicited by the researcher. In Rüdiger and Dayter's (2017) reflections on their study of an online pick-up artist community, they argue that, because the group is non-vulnerable, but exhibits hostile behaviour patterns, the most ethical and appropriate course of action for both researcher and researched was *not* to seek consent from these users. As explained earlier, however, I judged that seeking consent was appropriate in the case of this study. By doing so, I gave potential participants the power to decide for themselves whether, and how, they wanted their posts to be used for research purposes. The fact that some did explicitly withhold their consent illustrates the need to ask these questions. Posts by these individuals, and any reproduction of their posts, have not been included in this study (along with those of contributors who did not respond at all). These omissions were considered to be reasonable adjustments, both because Mumsnet threads do not tend to unfold in chronological sequence, and because participants often do not respond directly to one another. Both threads remained coherent overall and several interactional sequences could still be identified.

The practice of anonymizing digital data by either removing or pseudonymizing usernames, as well as any other details that may lead to the author's identification, such as names, places or geographical locations, is relatively commonplace in digital discourse studies (e.g. Jaworska, 2017 and Rüdiger and Dayter, 2017). Because I contacted contributors individually, I was able to give them a choice regarding their level of anonymity. Most participants chose to keep their original usernames, which shows that anonymization is not always the most favourable option, with some participants preferring to have their authorship acknowledged. However, some did opt to have their names changed, and have subsequently been given pseudonyms that retain the spirit of their original username. However, guaranteeing anonymity is unfortunately not a straightforward process when data are collected online because quotes can often be traced back to the original source through a web search (Androutsopoulos, 2008; Ess, 2007). The double measure of paraphrasing or altering quotes can provide absolute anonymity (Ess, 2007), but this option is not ideal in the context of sociolinguistic research such as this, where the most subtle linguistic choices may be of significant interest. The fact that I select threads only from the 'chat' section of Mumsnet Talk circumvents these issues to a large extent. Posts to this area are kept on the site only for a period of 90 days from the first post. As long as the data are shared more than 90 days from the date of first posting, quotes will therefore not be 'searchable' online, offering an additional safeguard. Although anonymity can never be absolutely guaranteed, it is therefore very likely that where participants in the Mumsnet study wished to remain anonymous, they will be.

Individual Mumsnet users were contacted through the Mumsnet private messaging system, a method chosen in collaboration with Mumsnet staff. In other digital contexts, contacting participants in this way may not be possible, making it very difficult to seek contributors' consent. In this case, it was generally an effective way of reaching out to Mumsnet users, although a few individuals did express annoyance at being contacted directly by a researcher. Messages to potential participants offered a brief summary of my research aims and provided a link to my personal blog, which included further information, as well as an extensive posting history that served to chart the development of this research over a period of approximately 18 months.[2] In both the message to potential participants and blog page, I introduced myself as not just a researcher but also 'a mother to a 4 and 5 year old'. By inviting users to read this blog, which included a great deal of personal and professional information, I also opened myself up to scrutiny, which helped to break down the unequal researcher/researched dichotomy. Both this willingness to be open and the emphasis on common ground between myself and my participants seemed to affect some Mumsnet users' willingness to trust me as a researcher. One participant, for example, explained and justified her consent in a private message by pointing to my status as a mother (and presumably also a woman), my political views and even my writing style (this interaction is discussed in more detail in Mackenzie, 2017b). As this example shows, communicating via private message was an effective way of reaching out to Mumsnet users, allowing them to engage in conversation, voice concerns and ask questions about the study – to have some sense that they were involved in the research process as participants rather than passive research 'subjects'. Informal discussions with participants also provided invaluable insights into their feelings and opinions about their involvement in the Talk forum and about their interactions being used in a research study, which further informed my developing understanding of the norms of interaction and information sharing within Mumsnet Talk.

Concluding remarks

This chapter has offered a transparent account of the Mumsnet study, focusing on the processes of data construction, identifying and analyzing discourses, and ethical decision-making. I have shown how I drew together qualitative methods associated with ethnography, grounded theory and linguistic discourse analysis as part of these processes. The value of self-reflexivity has been emphasized throughout, and I have shown how my personal reflections and engagement with the research site have influenced the research design and analysis.

The methodological insights presented in this chapter are of particular importance for two groups of researchers. First, they are useful for discourse studies scholars whose work seeks to pinpoint and scrutinize the discursive forces at play in people's everyday experiences and interactions. As noted earlier and in Chapter 2, there is a lack of clarity in this literature around what exactly discourses are, how they can be identified and how they operate in everyday practice. Following on from the introduction to discourses and feminist poststructuralist theory in Chapter 2, this chapter has contributed to research in this area by explicating the process of discourse analysis and identification in a clear and transparent way. Second, this chapter is useful for researchers of digital contexts who wish to take an emic perspective, but do not necessarily have direct or face-to-face contact with their research subjects or participants. By detailing the self-reflexive processes I engaged in, and showing how they informed my research design, analysis and ethical decision-making, I have offered practical insights for internet researchers who wish to conduct their research in an informed, context-sensitive way that minimizes the risk of harm to their participants or research subjects.

Chapters 5 and 6 will detail the results of the explorations that have been introduced in this chapter. They will focus on the two threads at the heart of this qualitative investigation, 'Your identity as a mother' and 'Can we have a child exchange?', considering how Mumsnet users are discursively positioned, and position themselves, within these interactions. These explorations begin in the following chapter, which will outline the eight discourses that have been identified through analysis of these threads. It will show how these discourses have been identified, the linguistic resources through which they are taken up and negotiated, and how they relate to broader socio-cultural norms around parenting and motherhood.

Notes

1 All extracts from Mumsnet Talk, both in this and subsequent chapters, are reproduced exactly as they are presented in the original discussions, with glosses added for acronyms. All extracts are reproduced with the permission of both the individual authors of the posts, and Mumsnet Limited. The majority of usernames are reproduced as in the original posts, but some are pseudonyms, at participants' requests
2 This blog is available at https://jaimack.wordpress.com.

5 Discourses of gendered parenthood in Mumsnet Talk[1]

In Chapter 2, I showed that powerful social forces have long worked to position parents in restrictive gendered subject positions that revolve around the ideal of the 'intensive' mother, who is expected to be the primary carer for her children, completely child-centred and self-sacrificing. I showed that expectations of women in western contexts have subtly shifted over time, with consumerism, for example, increasingly shaping the image of the 'good mother' in recent years, but that ideals about motherhood continue to be moulded by the core values of intensive motherhood. Scholarship has shown that these continuing expectations are highly problematic, making it difficult for parents to have equal access to caring and working practices, and restricting the scope of who and what is deemed 'good' parenting (and especially mothering). Explorations of gender, parenting and motherhood to date, however, have rarely been specific about *how* discourses such as 'intensive mothering' or 'child-centredness' operate in everyday life, what specific forms they take and how they merge and interrelate. This chapter works to address that gap.

The analysis and findings that are presented in this chapter are important for two primary reasons. First, they reveal eight discourses that capture key insights about the social norms, expectations and assumptions parents are navigating in a digital age. These discourses are named as 'gendered parenthood', 'child-centric motherhood', 'mother as main parent', 'absent fathers', 'commercialized motherhood', 'classed motherhood', 'equal parenting' and 'individuality'. Each section of this chapter introduces one of these discourses, detailing the forms of knowledge and subjectivity they produce, the power relations they inscribe, and some of the specific linguistic mechanisms through which they operate. I also show how each discourse both relates to and further specifies the nature of other discourses and themes identified in the wider literature. Second, the findings presented in this chapter are important because they emphasize the significance and pervasiveness of 'gendered parenthood', a discourse that is at once new, because it has not yet been specifically named, yet also established, because it underpins a range of other discourses and key themes around gender and parenthood that have been identified in the literature. I demonstrate that 'gendered parenthood' is an overarching discourse that produces, merges and competes with the further specific discourses that are outlined in each section, thus revealing that gender is central to the ways in which individuals can negotiate a position for themselves as parents within Mumsnet Talk. The chapter aims to expose and scrutinize the multiple ways in which discourses of gendered parenthood operate, and by doing so, to challenge the potentially restrictive gendered assumptions and expectations that dominate Mumsnet users' sense of what it means to be a parent and a mother in a digital age.

Gendered parenthood

'Gendered parenthood' is identified here as a discourse that works to fix individuals who are parents in distinct, binary subject positions along gendered lines: as mothers and fathers. It can be subsumed within the overarching discourse of 'gender differentiation', which positions 'men' and 'women' as separate and different (Baxter, 2003; see Chapter 2). Researchers across the social sciences have long been pointing to discourses that inscribe restrictive forms of knowledge about what is expected of 'mothers' and 'fathers', such as 'good mothering' and 'involved fatherhood' (Miller, 2007, 2011; see Chapter 2). However, none have yet named 'gendered parenthood' as an overarching discourse that captures and prevails across all of these discursive formations, in the same way that 'gender differentiation' underlines the persistent division of people as 'male' and 'female' across different spheres. Explicitly identifying and naming this discourse is important because doing so emphasizes the profoundly *gendered* ways in which forms of knowledge and subjectivity around parenthood are constructed and conceptualized within (and beyond) Mumsnet Talk. In this section, I show how this discourse of 'gendered parenthood' is manifested in the Mumsnet Talk threads 'Your identity as a mother' and 'Can we have a child exchange?', before outlining five further discourses of gendered parenthood in the sub-sections that follow. By identifying and analyzing these discourses and indicating the linguistic mechanisms through which they operate, I draw attention to some of the specific ways in which forms of knowledge about gender, parenthood and family life are produced, and individuals are positioned as gendered parental subjects.

For most contributors to the 'Your identity as a mother' thread, 'mum' seems to be the default subject position. This position is often taken up quite explicitly, towards the start of contributors' posts, through pronouns and categories. For example, in the following excerpts, contributors all employ some variation of the clause 'I am mum', where the personal pronoun 'I' is in the grammatical position of the subject and the category 'mum' or 'mother' is in the grammatical position of the complement, so that 'I' and 'mother' are equated directly.[2]

Post 4. *Loopylouu*. I've been a mother for so long
Post 12. *IdealistAndProudOfIt*. I'm a mum to 2 under5s
Post 72. *museumum*. I am 'mum' a lot of the time
Post 84. *Bedsheets4knickers*. I'm a mother of 2

Of course, it is not surprising that these contributors tend to take up the subject position 'mum', given the context in which they are interacting; the title of the Mumsnet website itself legitimizes 'mum/mother' as the obvious, common-sense subject position available to its users. It is therefore likely to be difficult for members of this site to completely escape the overarching discourse of 'gendered parenthood', although there *are* moments at which they take up other subject positions, such as the gender-neutral 'parent' or the individualistic 'I', which will be explored later in this chapter, in relation to the discourses of 'equal parenting' and 'individuality'.

A discourse of 'gendered parenthood' is also evident in the 'Can we have a child exchange?' thread, although it is not so immediately identifiable. In the foregoing examples, users take up *direct* indices of gender when they adopt the subject position mum/mother. In 'Can we have a child exchange?', participants do not self-identify in this way at all, but they can be said to use *indirect* indices of gender: resources that have come, through shared socio-cultural knowledge and repetition, to be associated with a particular group or identity (Ochs, 1992), such as mothers, Catholics or working class men. Gender and language research has offered insights as to what such linguistic and communicative indices of gender might look like. Holmes and Stubbe (2003: 574), for example, draw on the claims of early research in this field (e.g. Coates, 1988, 1996; Fishman, 1983; Holmes, 1984; Lakoff, 1975) when showing that a competitive, autonomous and referentially oriented style has tended to be culturally associated with masculinity, whereas an indirect, facilitative, collaborative and affectively oriented style has been tied to notions of femininity. 'Affective' behaviour and interactional styles have also been linked with western ideals of 'good' motherhood, which tend to position women as 'natural' carers and nurturers (Gillies, 2007; Lawler, 2000; Wall, 2010; see Chapter 2). Although such claims have been widely criticized for their simplistic and generalized polarization of 'men' and 'women' as opposites, who have predictable, fixed linguistic habits (Cameron, 1996; Cameron and Coates, 1989; Eckert and McConnell-Ginet,

1992), they continue to have currency in a contemporary context, offering a surprisingly accurate reflection of 'societal expectations and norms of appropriate gendered behaviour' (Mills and Mullany, 2011: 53).

Contributors to 'Can we have a child exchange?' can be said to index the cultural stereotype that women orient towards the expression of moods, feelings and attitudes in their talk, through their use of 'affectively oriented' resources (Holmes and Stubbe, 2003: 574). For example, contributors to 'Can we have a child exchange?' frequently deploy what Lakoff (1975: 13) calls 'empty' adjectives in descriptions of their children, using words such as 'charming', 'sweet', 'lovely', 'delightful' and 'cute' to describe them in positive, loving terms that 'express approbation in terms of one's own personal emotional reaction'. These resources are re-named here as *affective adjectives*, a term that more directly relates to their function and does not carry the same negative implications as Lakoff's original label. Contributors also make frequent use of intensifying adverbs, such as 'very', 'extremely', 'truly' and 'exceptionally', to emphasize the intensive nature of their feelings. Further, in the digital context of the Mumsnet Talk forum, contributors have various typographical resources at their disposal, including italics, bold, capitals, punctuation and emojis, which have often been linked with stereotypically 'feminine' interactional styles in new media research. For example, Wolf's (2000) research on US online newsgroups suggests that women use more emoticons than men to express emotion, solidarity, support and positive feelings, and Vaisman's (2013) study of Israeli blogs shows that users perform glamorous, desirable 'girliness' through play with font and typography, together with a range of other linguistic resources. The following excerpts are illustrative of participants' affective style when describing their children in the 'Can we have a child exchange?' thread, through their use of a range of affectively oriented resources.

Post 4.   *ChaosTrulyReigns*. I've got am extremely useful 11yo DD [11-year-old darling daughter[3]]. Reason for swap? 3 gazillion wayward loom bands that she **needs** inhher possession at all times.

Post 11. *RoseberryTopping*. he's lovely to snuggle and smells nice ☺

Post 44. *SheWhoDaresGins*. **PLEASE SOMEBODY TAKE MY 5 YR OLD DS [darling son] BEFORE MY HEAD EXPLODES WITH HIS CONSTANT CHATTERING!!!!**

Post 58. *WhispersofWickedness*. She is VERY cute though ☺

The pervasiveness of an affectively oriented style across the 'Can we have a child exchange?' thread can be said to both draw upon and reinforce the indexical ties between femininity, motherhood and affective behaviour (especially towards children). If contributors and readers recognize these ties, the adoption of this style will position the authors as *female* parents: as mothers, who are describing their children in a way that is consistent with cultural expectations of women and mothers, particularly in a western context. This claim, however, is a tentative one: indirectly indexical resources, by their very nature, cannot be exclusively linked to one social function or subject position, and they are likely to rely on local, as well as more global, meanings and assumptions (Agha, 2007; Bucholtz, 2009; Johnstone and Kiesling, 2008). Contributors' use of what I describe here as an 'affectively oriented' style may therefore be interpreted in different ways, since 'femininity' and 'good motherhood' are not oriented around emotions, personal connections and sensitivity for all people at all times. It may be, for example, that contributors use these resources primarily to emphasize their love for and personal responses to their children, as I will suggest in my exploration of the discourse of 'child-centric motherhood', ahead. The variable and context-dependent nature of indexical meanings, both in general and in the 'Can we have a child exchange?' thread, is explored in more detail in Mackenzie (2017a). Another important consideration here is that contributors may orient to the gendered connotations of these resources in an ironic and subversive way. This interpretation would certainly be consistent with the playful, humorous tone of the thread (see further discussion ahead and in Chapter 6).

Mumsnet users' adoption of direct and indirect indices of gender in both discussions of their parental identities and descriptions of their children is a key indicator that 'gendered parenthood' is a central, dominant discourse in the two threads explored here. Five further discourses of gendered parenthood, which rely on the differentiation of parents in gendered terms before further positioning them in specific ways, are outlined in the sections that follow.

Mother as main parent and absent fathers

'Mother as main parent' and 'absent fathers' are identified here as separate discourses that often form a complementary pair because the forms of knowledge and subjectivity that they produce work to reinforce one another, inscribing oppositional, unequal power relations between men and women who are parents. Through the positioning of mothers as 'main parents', who have primary responsibility for their children, fathers are positioned, by implication, as secondary parents. When fathers are absent, completely excluded from the family sphere, women's position as the 'main parent' is reinforced. The identification of these discourses is consistent with the 'common-sense' assumption that women are the 'natural', primary carers for children. It also echoes Sunderland's (2000, 2004) identification of a 'part-time father/mother as main parent' combination discourse, introduced in Chapter 2, which positions mothers as the parent with primary responsibility for a child's upbringing, and fathers in a supporting role. There are two key distinctions, however, between the pair of discourses identified here, and by Sunderland (2000, 2004). First, the 'absent fathers' discourse emphasizes the way fathers are often not just positioned as 'part-time' parents but also completely excluded from parental subject positions in Mumsnet Talk interactions. This discourse is therefore identified through close attention to *absences* in the text; to what (or in this case, who) could have been, but is not, present (Sunderland, 2000; van Leeuwen, 1995, 1996; see discussion in Chapters 2 and 4). The second distinction is that I name 'mother as main parent' and 'absent fathers' as separate discourses, rather than a combination discourse, even though they persistently merge with and affirm one another in the threads analyzed here. I do this because the 'mother as main parent' discourse can still be evidenced even where fathers are very much present in an interaction. Naming these discourses separately also facilitates an analysis of the positioning of men and fathers in their own right, not just in relation to what they reveal about the positioning of women and mothers. Thus, I allow space for a wider range of perspectives, including those that are relatively marginalized in these interactions. This section demonstrates some of the linguistic mechanisms through which the 'mother as main parent' and 'absent fathers' discourses operate in the Mumsnet Talk threads. As with 'gendered parenthood', these discourses are identified largely through close scrutiny of referential devices, especially pronouns.

The 'mother as main parent' and 'absent fathers' discourses operate most persistently through the continual elision of men and fathers in both 'Your identity as a mother' and 'Can we have a child exchange?', in which there are very few references to fathers, or indeed any other male adults. The absence of men and fathers is particularly marked in the 'Your identity as a mother' thread. The title and opening post of this thread (Extract 5.1) very clearly set out pandarific's concern with *women's* parental identities, as *mothers*.

Extract 5.1 Opening post from 'Your identity as a mother'[2]

pandarific Sun 01-Jun-14 14:43:17

1. I've been reading a lot of fiction that deals with motherhood and
2. family relationships and I'm curious as to how it changes people,
3. and their view of themselves. Has your perception of who you
4. are changed since you had children? How much of your identity
5. is bound up with being a mum? Do you think the strength of

6. your desire to be a mum/what stage in your life you had them
7. affected the degree of the changes?

8. For some reason this has come out reading like an exam question
9. – it's not meant to be! Just curious about people's experiences.

In pandarific's direct appeals to the reader, her use of gender-specific references to 'mother' and 'mum', together with the second-person pronouns 'you' and 'your', presupposes that her readers are all female parents, thus constraining the parameters for appropriate participation in this thread. Unsurprisingly, all contributors to this thread subsequently *do* present themselves as women, and most as mothers (although some do not adopt the subject position mum/ mother, identifying themselves instead as 'parents', or someone who 'has children'). They also reply to the direct second-person address of the opening post, by and large, with a proliferation of first-person singular pronouns such as 'I', 'me' and 'my'. A brief look at pronoun references across the whole thread (Tables 5.1 and 5.2) shows that this is a recurring pattern.

The figure of 941 singular references to the self in this thread is particularly striking when set against the number of 9 singular references to men, or 14 plural references to the contributor *with* a man, demonstrating the absence of men quite vividly. It may of course be the case that there *are* no male carers in some contributors' lives; as mentioned in Chapter 3, the details of participants' backgrounds and circumstances are not known, beyond what is

Table 5.1 Pronouns referring to the self and/or other women in 'Your identity as a mother'

First-person singular pronouns 'I', 'me', 'my'	Third-person singular feminine pronouns 'she', 'her' referencing a female carer	First-person plural pronouns 'we', 'our', 'ourselves' including the author and other mums/ Mumsnet users	Third-person singular feminine pronouns 'she', 'her' referencing a daughter
941	27	16	15

Table 5.2 Pronouns referring to men in 'Your identity as a mother'

Third-person singular masculine pronouns 'he', 'him', 'his' referencing a male carer	First-person plural pronouns 'we', 'our', 'ourselves' including the author and a male carer	Third-person singular masculine pronouns 'he', 'him', 'his' referencing a son
9	14	11

presented in their posts. Nevertheless, this is a marked absence, pointing to either an actual absence of male carers or a presence that is not acknowledged in these posts.

Many posts to 'Your identity as a mother', such as the one written by cakesonatrain (Extract 5.2), almost exclusively employ first-person singular pronouns. This pattern often implies that the contributor has total responsibility for their children, and either points to the absence or disregards the potential existence of any other parent or carer. Cakesonatrain's use of the gendered terms 'breastfeeding' (rather than, for example, the gender-neutral 'feeding') and 'Mumming' (as opposed to 'parenting') in lines 2-3 also works to exclude male carers by constituting these tasks as gender-specific – integral to the role of 'mum'.

Extract 5.2 Post 3 from 'Your identity as a mother' (first-person singular pronouns in bold – my emphasis)

cakesonatrain Sun 01-Jun-14 15:07:15

1. **I** think **I** am almost entirely Mum. **My** dc [darling children] are
2. still both under 3 so there's a lot of physical Mumming to do,
3. with breastfeeding, nappies, carrying, bathing etc. **I** don't know if
4. it will be less intense when they're older, and **I** might let myself
5. be a bit more **Me** again, but right now **I** am almost refusing to
6. have an identity beyond Mum. **I** am a bit 'old **Me**' at work, but
7. **I**'m part time now so there's less of that too.

The predominance of first-person singular pronouns and participants' self-categorization as 'mums' in the 'Your identity as a mother' thread, together with other linguistic strategies that exclude men as parents, is not surprising given pandarific's exclusive emphasis on female parents in the title and opening post, and the website's target audience. But there are several recurring statements that could logically break away from this singular emphasis on mothers, challenging the terms of the opening post. For example, within the clause 'I have children', which recurs in various forms across the thread, such as 'I am expecting my first' (post 85), the singular pronoun 'I' could easily be replaced with the plural 'we' or 'our', incorporating reference to the self and a second parent with little change to the content of the post. An alternative expression of this sentiment that can be found in post 9, 'we have only one child', shows that it *is* possible to challenge the terms of the opening post whilst still offering a relevant response, through the use of plural pronoun reference.

The patterns of pronoun use in 'Your identity as a mother' imply that contributors to this thread have total responsibility for their children, whilst men are, by and large, erased as potentially relevant parental subjects. It does not seem to be the case, either, that men are absent from this thread because participants share parental responsibilities with female carers, such as female co-parents or other family members: where other carers *are* made relevant, they are always male. Overall, it can be said that the linguistic patterns of reference in this thread both position contributors within the 'mother as main parent' discourse, as the main (or even sole) carers for their children, and point to a discourse of exclusion, 'absent fathers'. These discourses frequently intersect, merging with and reinforcing one another.

It is important to note that men and fathers are not completely absent from the 'Your identity as a mother' thread. On the rare occasions that they are made relevant, however, contributors often position themselves and their male partners as different and oppositional subjects, as MorningTimes does in post 19 (Extract 5.3).

Extract 5.3 Post 19 from 'Your identity as a mother'

MorningTimes Sun 01-Jun-14 20:29:39

1. I agree with **cakes** – I feel as if I am 99% 'mum' at the moment! I
2. know it will pass though, I am a SAHM [stay-at-home-mum]
3. and am looking after three preschool DC [darling children] all
4. day (plus a fourth who is at school during the day) so I just don't
5. have the time or the energy to be anyone else at the moment.

6. DH [darling husband] does a lot with the children too but at least
7. he has a separate identity because he is out at work and mixes
8. with other people there.

9. I also struggle to spend time away from the DC for more than a
10. night though. I have friends who will happily go abroad on
11. holiday without their DC but I just wouldn't want to do that.

In this post, MorningTimes employs a range of pronouns and categories that constitute herself and her husband as distinct and separate subjects, within an overarching discourse of 'gendered parenthood'. For example, she begins each of the three paragraphs of her post with a singular pronoun or noun phrase: 'I' (line 1), 'DH' (darling husband; line 6) and 'I' (line 9), which creates a clear graphological separation between the main subject of each paragraph. She also uses exclusively singular pronouns when referring to herself or her husband (never the more inclusive 'we'), positioning herself and her 'DH' as separate individuals, rather than a joint unit. Furthermore, MorningTimes's self-positioning in a fixed, gendered parental role – as a 'mum' – through the relational clauses 'I am 99% "mum"' (line 1) and 'I am a SAHM' (line 2) contrasts with her positioning of her husband as someone who undertakes parental activities – who 'does a lot with the children' (line 6), but does not take up a parental subject position. The acronym 'SAHM' (stay-at-home-mum), further, positions her in the private sphere ('at home'), whereas she positions her husband in an opposing 'work' space. MorningTimes therefore positions herself as the 'main parent', whose status as a parent determines who she *is*, whereas her husband's determines only what he *does*. This polarized representation of male and female parents is not unusual in the 'Your identity as a mother' thread as a whole. Where contributors do make reference to men, they are often positioned as different and separate, and it is the contributors, as mothers, who are fixed in a parental subjectivity – as the 'main' parents.

Child-centric motherhood

The persistence of social expectations about maternal 'child-centredness' has long been established in sociological research, and sometimes named as a pervasive discourse in western contexts (Wall, 2013; see Chapter 2). This section reveals some of the specific ways in which a discourse of 'child-centric motherhood' works to position Mumsnet users as mothers who are both completely devoted and defined by their relation to their children, integrating the positions of the 'child-centred' and the 'total' mother (the way these positions merge is explicated in Chapter 4). I focus, unlike most literature that deals with the theme of maternal child-centredness and sacrifice, on the ways in which a discourse of 'child-centric motherhood' restricts women's access to a range of subject positions, by positioning them in relation to their children to the exclusion of all other potential roles and relations with others.

The exclusivity of the 'child-centric mother' subject position can be contrasted with the more flexible 'mother' subject position that is offered within a discourse of 'gendered parenthood'. For example, in post 102 of 'Your identity as a mother', Thurlow positions herself within a discourse of 'gendered parenthood' when she identifies herself as a female parent in the statement '*I am a mum*, a worker, a partner, a daughter and a friend' (my emphasis). However, she also takes up other subject positions here: as a worker, partner, daughter and friend. In post 13 of the same thread, Crazym also takes up a discourse of 'gendered parenthood' when she states that '*being a mum is just a part of who I am*, not the whole' (my emphasis). In these statements, both contributors conceptualize their identity as consisting of many 'parts', showing that a discourse of 'gendered parenthood' does not completely close down all possible ways of being an individual for them. As I will show in this section, however, a discourse of 'child-centric motherhood' *does* more dramatically limit the subject positions available to female parents.

The distinction between 'gendered parenthood' and 'child-centric motherhood' can be clarified by examining contributors' use of intensifiers in the following excerpts from 'Your identity as a mother'. Here, intensifiers such as '100%' and 'almost entirely' (highlighted in bold) suggest that these users' relation to their children, as *mothers*, has total (or very near total) influence over their sense of self, is the *only* subject position available to them, and works to exclude them from all other subjectivities.

Post 3. *cakesonatrain*. I think I am **almost entirely** Mum.

Post 11. *EggNChips*. As soon as I became a mum, I was **100%** mum and loved it. . .

Post 16. *cakesonatrain*. I am **almost wholly** Mum,

Post 18. *Kath6151*. I have been **so intensely** mum for the last 10 months

There are also other ways in which contributors to 'Your identity as a mother' are positioned as 'child-centric', 'total' mothers. In the following excerpts, for example, the category 'good mums' (highlighted in bold) evaluates women in relation to their successful adoption of the subject position 'mum'. The implication with both uses of this category is that 'good mums' devote themselves to their children and to the role of 'mother'. The negative construction 'good mums don't. . .' and the bald, unmitigated statement 'that's what's important' work to imply that women's positioning as child-centric mothers is imperative and fixed – that they do not have a choice but to be positioned in this way.

Post 59. *Viglioso*. **good mums** don't, apparently, wear make-up: that money/time could be spent on PFB [precious first-born]

Post 66. *MrsPennyapple*. Last night he responded with 'but you're a **good mum**, and that's what's important'.

A third way in which Mumsnet users are positioned as 'child-centric mothers' is through the implication that their children's needs come first, whilst their own needs are secondary. This is an established trope of 'intensive motherhood' (see Chapter 2) that is apparent in the excerpts from posts 59 and 66 of 'Your identity as a mother' that were presented earlier. Several contributors to 'Can we have a child exchange?' also position themselves as 'child-centric' mothers through the implication that their children's needs come before their own. In post 17 (Extract 5.4), for example, MrsKoala describes her son as the instigator of quite violent actions, which she seems to passively accept.

Extract 5.4 Post 17 from 'Can we have a child exchange?'

MrsKoala Wed 16-Jul-14 14:09:26

1. I'll take anything in return for my non sleeping, climbing 22mo
2. [month old] with a snotty cold. Recent hobbies include: Biting
3. your head. Insisting you lay on the floor while he covers you in
4. cushions then using your head as a trampoline. Taking off his
5. nappy and doing a poo somewhere random in the house,
6. smearing it over himself and everything while saying cheerily 'a
7. mess' and 'i did'.

Many of the processes MrsKoala attributes to her child imply negative evaluations, such as 'biting', which connotes aggression and animalistic behaviour, 'insisting', which suggests the child is controlling and force-ful, and 'smearing', which has negative implications of irrevocable and far-reaching damage. These negative evaluations could in one sense work to distance MrsKoala from her child; nevertheless, she still presents her child's needs and whims as coming before her own. By positioning herself as a passive participant in her interactions with her son, she appears willing to suffer the negative consequences of his actions: being bitten, jumped on and having to clean up faeces from her child and her house. Her passive role is further emphasized through her marked use of the second-person pronouns 'your' and 'you' in reference to herself, where 'my' and 'I' would be more conventional. This use of pronouns works to distance MrsKoala from the situation she describes, further removing her from any agentic role in this interaction with her son. MrsKoala's words therefore work to position her as a child-centric mother who makes sacrifices for her child, even as she emphasizes the negative impact his actions have on her life.

Similarly, in post 18 of 'Can we have a child exchange?' (Extract 5.5), nordibird also takes up the 'child-centric motherhood' discourse by posi-tioning herself as a passive participant in her interactions with her child.

Extract 5.5 Post 18 from 'Can we have a child exchange?'

nordibird Wed 16-Jul-14 14:12:50

1. I'll take the teenagers, will they fit in our spare room? I'd be
2. perfect, I'm up to speed on the Hunger Games and stuff.

3. In exchange I'm offering a seven-month-old who'll only sleep on
4. you – perfect for anyone who misses baby snuggles! Will eat

5. anything. Warning: Not suitably for anyone with back or neck
6. problems.

Here, nordibird offers for (mock) exchange 'a seven-month-old who'll only sleep on you' (lines 3-4). The negative implications of having a child 'who'll only sleep on you' will be apparent to most, and she alludes to one problem in her closing statement 'Warning: Not suitably for anyone with back or neck problems' (lines 5-6). Yet nordibird frames this trait in positive terms with her (presumably tongue-in-cheek) claim that this child is 'perfect for anyone who misses baby snuggles!' (line 4). Like MrsKoala, nordibird appears willing to suffer negative consequences in order to meet her child's needs. Both participants' complaints and negative evaluations of their children, although they are veiled by humour and irony, suggest that they resist being positioned as 'child-centric mothers' in any straightforward way. However, as in MrsKoala's post, nordibird's acceptance of these consequences draws attention to the difficulty of escaping the 'child-centric motherhood' discourse, which works to position participants in relation to their children throughout both of the threads analyzed here, even where they try to resist it.

Finally, the 'child-centric motherhood' discourse can be identified through Mumsnet users' detailed descriptions of their children in the 'Can we have a child exchange?' thread. Through these descriptions, the authors of these posts position themselves exclusively in relation to their children: any sense of who participants are is gained through an impression of who *their children* are. As the thread develops, contributors' descriptions and evaluations come together to construct an image of the 'perfect child', who is intelligent and/or ambitious, has a special skill, is clean, tidy and generally useful or helpful, has a pleasant disposition, is funny or entertaining, attractive and affectionate. Contributors also frequently use affective adjectives, such as 'lovely' and 'delightful', and intensifying adverbs, such as 'utterly', to describe their children in positive terms. Such positive evaluations work to position participants as proud, loving parents who celebrate their children's qualities and achievements: as child-centric mothers. The nature of the descriptions that are presented in 'Can we have a child exchange?' is further elaborated both in the section that follows and in Chapter 6.

Commercialized motherhood

Posts to the 'Can we have a child exchange?' thread tend to adopt a relatively uniform style and structure, with participants introducing their children, describing their qualities and 'offering' them for exchange. These posts mimic classified advertisements: short written advertisements, often written by private sellers of second-hand goods, that are traditionally found in the 'classified' section of print newspapers. The classified advertisement genre is very much out of place in the Mumsnet Talk discussion forum; the idea of exchanging or selling children is extremely subversive and incongruous with Mumsnet's goals of pooling knowledge, advice and support for parents (Mumsnet Limited, 2017). The genre of classified advertisements therefore serves, in this context, as a 'frame' (Goffman, 1974) that governs the organization and shape of participants' interactions, but without any expectation that the usual outcomes of classified advertisements will occur. This is a process of transposition that Goffman (1974) calls 'keying'.

By keying the classified advertisement frame in 'Can we have a child exchange?', contributors create a humorous, ironic tone that makes multiple layers of interpretation possible. These effects are explored in detail in Chapter 6, where I focus on the way contributors to this thread negotiate discourses of gendered parenthood through play and collective alignment. In this section, however, I focus on one layer of meaning in posts to this thread, considering how Mumsnet users' engagement in the faux promotion of their children for exchange or sale superimposes a commercial perspective on motherhood, women and their relation to children. This perspective can be seen to operate in the excerpts presented ahead, where contributors draw on the linguistic conventions of classified advertisements to 'offer' their children for exchange and describe their defining 'features'.

> Post 1. *BertieBotts*. Reads most things. Speaks some German. Quite helpful around the house.
> Post 4. *ChaosTrulyReigns*. I've got am extremely useful 11yo DD [11-year-old darling daughter]
> Post 37. *Wilberforce2*. I can offer a lovely 4.5 month old baby girl who is getting desperate to eat
> Post 73. *InanimateCarbonRod*. Total bookworm, very sporty and is a Minecraftaholic.

In posts 4 and 37, the child is introduced in an extended noun phrase. Participants' use of the indefinite articles 'a' and 'an' de-emphasizes any relationship between author and child (where a personal pronoun such as 'my', for example, would emphasize this relationship). Their referential strategies, too, create distance from the child: the categories 'baby girl' and '11yo', for example, make no reference to the relationship between author and child, where a category such as 'daughter' or 'son' (usually conventionalized in the acronyms DD and DS) would. Positive and evaluative adjectives, such as 'lovely' and 'extremely [useful]', are more personal, but their intensifying function also emphasizes the competitive element of these posts, which is prominent in most promotional genres (Bhatia, 2005). In posts 1 and 73, participants again distance themselves from the children they describe, this time by listing their attributes and through elision of the subject, which work to position children in terms of their valuable assets, rather than through, for example, their names or their relation to the author.

The linguistic conventions of classified advertisements that are present in the foregoing excerpts work, on one level, to commodify children, positioning them as objects for sale. The way children are objectified and competitively pitted against one another in these descriptions also captures the *business* element of this mock exchange – the framing of the thread as a sales opportunity, with contributors showing off their children's talents (as well as lamenting their flaws) under the guise of promoting their children as products. The keying of the classified advertisement frame in this thread may be playful, but in light of claims that consumerist values are increasingly shaping contemporary mothering practices (see Chapter 2), these interactions can also be read as engaging with a discourse of 'commercialized motherhood'. This discourse positions mothers as the 'producers' of children as commodities and children as the 'products' of this endeavour. In particular, contributors can be said to play with the concept of the 'good' mother, who (as explained in Chapter 2) is constituted as both entirely responsible for the outcomes of her children's lives (here, their 'value' as 'products') and using all resources at her disposal to maximize these outcomes. In this way, a close interplay between the discourses of 'commercialized' and 'child-centric' motherhood can be identified in this thread, an intersection that will be further explored in the sections that follow. Contributors' allusion to the expectations of 'good mothers' through humorous play gives their posts a subversive edge that allows them to be read as a critique of such expectations; this layer of meaning will be further explored in Chapter 6.

Classed motherhood

The final discourse of gendered parenthood that is presented here, 'classed motherhood', works to position women in both classed *and* gendered parental subject positions – for example as 'middle class', 'working class' or 'upper class' mothers. This discourse is identified through an examination of resources that are indirectly indexical of class in contributions to the 'Can we have a child exchange?' thread. As explained at the start of Chapter 5, indirect indices are resources that have come to be associated with a particular group or identity (Ochs, 1992). Participants' use of 'affectively oriented' resources in descriptions of their children, for example, can index cultural stereotypes around femininity and motherhood. In this section, I show that contributors to 'Can we have a child exchange?' also frequently draw on linguistic and cultural resources that can be said to index sociocultural expectations, assumptions and stereotypes around 'middle class' identities in descriptions of their children.

Several decades of sociological research, mostly conducted in a British context, have demonstrated strong links between access to particular sociocultural resources and belonging to classed categories (e.g. Abercrombie and Warde, 2003; Bourdieu, 1984; Giddens, 1981; Goldthorpe, 1980; Parkin, 1982; Savage, Cunningham, Devine, Friedman, Laurison, McKenzie, Miles, Snee and Wakeling, 2015). Table 5.3 summarizes some of these enduring findings and assumptions about class, and what constitutes membership of a particular class. It presents class distinctions on a sliding scale, from what have been called the 'lower' or 'working' class to the 'middle classes' and the 'upper' class. These categories emerged during the period of the industrial revolution and have endured to this day, despite numerous attempts (e.g. Goldthorpe, 1980; Savage et al., 2015) to develop and expand them. This table shows that access to resources such as wealth, educational opportunity and 'highbrow' cultural activities has tended to be firmly linked with a (predominantly British) 'middle class' identity. These resources can be conceptualized as indices because they are likely to be salient in terms of everyday assumptions and stereotypes about what it means to belong to a particular classed category. As noted in relation to 'gendered parenthood', however, it remains problematic to draw conclusions about the way individuals are orienting towards particular identities on the basis of such variables.

As noted in Chapter 2, the social construction of motherhood has long been linked with notions of class and classed categories, with scholars such as Lawler (2000), Miller (2007) and Wall (2010), following Hays (1996), suggesting that 'middle class' values are closely tied to ideals of the 'good mother'. The fact that Mumsnet, the most popular and successful parenting website in the UK, is perceived as a site that is both dominated by middle class users and works to reinforce ties between middle class values and 'good' mothering practices (Pedersen and Smithson, 2010, 2013) adds weight to these claims. In the paragraphs that follow, I show how social expectations around class and classed identities can feed into Mumsnet users' interactions.

Throughout the 'Can we have a child exchange?' thread, contributors draw on a number of linguistic and cultural resources that can be conceptualized

Table 5.3 Social indices of class, based on sociological research[1]

	Lower/working class	Middle classes	Upper class
Occupation	Waged, unskilled, manual	Salaried, professional and management; self-employed/small business ownership; occupation more significant than wealth	Salaried, professional and management; self-employed/large business ownership
Property	Rental in homes with low value, neighbourhoods with low 'market attractiveness' (Savage et al., 2015)	Likely ownership of homes with middle to high value, in neighbourhoods with middle to high 'market attractiveness'	Ownership of (multiple) homes with very high value, in neighbourhoods with very high 'market attractiveness'
Wealth	Very low income, little or no accumulated wealth	Middle to high income, some accumulated wealth	Very high income, and/or significant inherited/ accumulated wealth; wealth more significant than occupation
Education	Compulsory, state education only, few qualifications	University and possibly private school education, numerous qualifications	Likely educated at prestigious and/or private institutions, such as Eton and Cambridge (Abercrombie and Warde, 2003), numerous qualifications
Cultural interests	Restricted engagement with leisure and cultural activities that are socially and institutionally approved and legitimized, or 'highbrow' (Bourdieu, 1984; Savage et al., 2015)	Engagement with a wide range of leisure and cultural activities, sometimes 'highbrow'	Engagement with a wide range of leisure and cultural activities, often 'highbrow'
Social networks	Restricted social networks; mainly familial ties	More diverse social networks; friendship, business and educational ties	Strong, mutually beneficial networks, based on familial, business, friendship and acquaintance ties: often called the 'old boy network' (Abercrombie and Warde, 2003)

Notes:[1] Collated from Goldthorpe (1980), Parkin (1971), Abercrombie and Warde (2003), Savage et al. (2015), Giddens (1981) and Bourdieu (1984).

as indices of a broadly, and typically British, 'middle class' identity. For example, in post 66 to 'Can we have a child exchange?' (Extract 5.6), PrincessLizzie uses formal, sophisticated linguistic resources with an apparent ease that suggests she has inherited a particular combination of institutionally legitimized cultural and educational capital whereby, from a young age, the resources available to her at home would have been supported and reinforced in an educational context, and vice versa (Bourdieu, 1984). It is important to note, however, that the playful and humorous tone of the thread continues in this post, again creating multiple possible layers of meaning that both go beyond and potentially subvert such assumptions around class. These meanings will be further explored in Chapter 6.

Extract 5.6 Post 66 from 'Can we have a child exchange?'

PrincessLizzie Wed 16-Jul-14 22:08:00

1. I offer five-year-old Lego addicts. Their days are spent
2. accidentally breaking apart fiendishly complex Lego
3. constructions and wailing for help in reconstruction, as their
4. ability to see what to do and understand Lego instructions is
5. greater than their ability to accomplish it, due to lack of
6. coordination. Can be relied on for a copious supply of riotous
7. giggling over nothing.

The complex sentence that comes between lines 1 and 6 exemplifies the kind of grammatical structures that are used in this thread. This construction can be divided into multiple clauses that are both paratactic and hypotactic, several of which also have very complex internal structures, such as 'accidentally breaking apart fiendishly complex Lego constructions' (lines 2–3), which ends with the heavily pre-modified noun phrase 'fiendishly complex Lego constructions'. This post also includes formal and sophisticated lexical items, such as 'fiendishly' (line 2), 'reconstruction' (line 3), 'copious' and 'riotous' (line 6). Similar words can be found across the thread, as shown in the following excerpts (see bold highlights):

Post 49. *Janez.* [H]e would . . . be as happy as a pig in the **proverbial** shit 😁
Post 50. *BertieBotts.* have v hilarious delusions . . .
Post 73. *InanimateCarbonRod.* Will swap for squish new born due to **rampant** broodiness

In many cases, words like these are positioned alongside linguistic and typographical resources that are rather more everyday and informal, such as 'shit' (post 49), 'squish[y]' (post 73), emoticons (post 49), strikethrough text (post 50) and abbreviations such as 'v' for 'very' (post 50). Such juxtapositions display contributors' ability to draw on a diverse range of resources in the negotiation of a style that is extremely well matched to the context of this specific Mumsnet Talk thread. In other words, the resources they use can be seen to index a particular background at times, but they also satisfy a number of other functions: to create a humorous exchange, to share stories about their children and to echo a shared style within this forum (the nature and importance of this shared style will be further detailed in Chapter 6). That participants' posts can capture this range of functions is, in itself, quite a striking demonstration of the extensive communicative resources they have at their disposal and the sophisticated ways in which they are able to deploy these resources.

Many contributors to the 'Can we have a child exchange?' thread also draw on economic and cultural resources in descriptions of their children. For example, in Excerpt 5.7, participants emphasize their children's various skills, talents, academic successes and intelligence (see bold highlights).

*Extract 5.7 Excerpts from 'Can we have a child exchange?':
posts 52, 55 and 87*

52. Clobbered Wed 16-Jul-14 20:49:07

1. Model 1: Twenty-one, driver, non-smoker, **recent graduate**.
2. Self-caring but tendency to wake early and pace the floor.

3. Model 2: Twenty, **excellent cook and percussionist**. Extreme
4. clothing abuse (floordrobe currently occupying 2 rooms of the
5. house) . . .

55. 2kidsintow Wed 16-Jul-14 21:16:47

1. I have on offer one 13 yo DD [13-year-old darling daughter].
2. She's very clean and tidy and has been known to clean down the
3. kitchen, empty the dishwasher and make a batch of choc chip
4. cookies if bored after school. Her sausage rolls are also amazing.

5. At most other times she is to be found **sitting with pen in hand,**
6. or **typing away on her novel** . . .

87. Timeisawastin Thu 17-Jul-14 00:36:29

1. I have on offer one 15yr old teenage girl. She's lovely, she's
2. bright, chatty and well-behaved. She's also **training her voice in**
3. **classical soprano singing**. All day. Every day. Non-stop.

By drawing attention to their children's intelligence and ambition in examples such as 'recent graduate' and 'typing away on her novel', participants position themselves as parents who are able to provide their children with opportunities to succeed in academic and workplace arenas: who have access to a wealth of cultural and economic resources and opportunities. Going to university and learning to play an instrument, for example, are both likely to involve significant financial investments. The fact that these participants refer to their children's interests in opera singing and playing musical instruments also points to the cultural resources at their disposal. These Mumsnet users' references to culturally 'highbrow' activities (Bourdieu, 1984), like novel writing or classical singing, are deployed with what Savage et al. (2015: 98) call a 'cultural confidence' that is characteristic of 'privileged' people. The casual ease with which such references are added to a list of other skills or qualities suggests, for example, that being a 'recent graduate' is no more striking a quality than being a 'non-smoker'; that writing a novel is as everyday, for these contributors' children, as cleaning the kitchen.

Overall, a discourse of 'classed motherhood' can be seen to constitute motherhood as not only a gendered and commercialized but also a *classed* endeavour in the 'Can we have a child exchange?' thread. This discourse intersects with the other discourses that have been introduced so far to the extent that it is difficult, at times, to disentangle them from one another. What emerges instead is a construction of motherhood that takes in all of these elements. This interdiscursivity, and the effects it creates, is further explored in the section that follows.

Intersecting discourses of gendered parenthood: constituting the 'good mother'

There are key moments in the Mumsnet Talk threads at which the discourses of gendered parenthood that have been introduced so far can be seen to intersect. In this section, I present some of these moments, showing how several discourses of gendered parenthood can merge to produce the 'good mother' subject position in both 'Can we have a child exchange?' and 'Your identity as a mother'.

A number of the discourses that have been identified so far in this chapter are at play in MicrobatSister's post to 'Can we have a child exchange?', which is reproduced in Extract 5.8.

Extract 5.8 Post 51 from 'Can we have a child exchange?'

MicrobatSister wed 16-Jul-14 20:34:37

1. I have on offer an 8.5 yr [year] old DS [darling son], who is
2. lovely and kindhearted, but can talk about Minecraft for at least
3. an hour before pausing for breath. He also wishes to become a
4. virologist when he grows up, and has (in his mind, anyway)
5. recently invented a cure for the common cold, which he also
6. natters endlessly on and on and on about. He is trying to rope me
7. in to getting him a market stall (a precursor to him having a
8. chain of stores – or is it better to just sell the recipe for millions
9. instead, Mummy?) and helping him sell it! Has a voice like a
10. FOGHORN, even his 'whispering' can be heard in the street
11. outside. Does sleep very well though.

12. Alternatively, I have DS2 [second darling son] – who is 2 next
13. week. Looks utterly angelic –blonde, big blue eyes, very
14. cuddly. But again, voice like a FOGHORN, like a duracell
15. bunny, just starting the whole tantrums phase, and STILL
16. wakes 4–5 times a night!

17. Willing to swap for any silent, monosyllabic or grunting
18. teenagers who enjoy staying in their rooms a lot. Don't care if
19. they can make tea or not as long as they sleep lots! 😬

In this post, MicrobatSister can be said to position herself within a discourse of 'gendered parenthood', as a *female* parent, by drawing on resources that are indexical of femininity in the descriptions of her children. These include the intensifying adverbs 'utterly' (line 13) and 'very' (lines 11 and 13) and the affective adjectives 'lovely' (line 2), 'angelic' (line 13) and 'cuddly' (line 14). MicrobatSister also uses capital letters for affective emphasis, drawing attention to her negative personal reaction to her son's behaviour with her capitalization of 'FOGHORN' (lines 10 and 14) and 'STILL' (line 15). Other descriptions point to a discourse of 'classed motherhood'. For example, she emphasizes her family's access to economic resources in the statement 'He also wishes to become a virologist when he grows up, and has . . . recently invented a cure for the common cold' (lines 3-5). Here, she implicitly suggests that her child has access to a good education and is likely to enter a very well-paid profession that will entail years of university education, whilst positioning herself as someone who has access to a range of cultural and economic resources to support this path. Her formal and sometimes technical lexical choices, such as 'virologist' (line 4) and 'wishes to become. . .' (line 3), which might have been phrased more simply as 'wants to study viruses', display an assured grasp of specialist and formal vocabulary that would be highly valued in educational and professional spheres. MicrobatSister's lengthy descriptions also commodify her children, labelling them for offer in terms of their desirable qualities, skills and virtues and thus positioning them within a discourse of 'commercialized motherhood', as 'products' of her parenting. Further, she draws on the 'child-centric motherhood' discourse through her consistent focus on her children and through positive evaluations, such as 'lovely and kindhearted' (line 2) and 'utterly angelic' (line 13). Like MrsKoala and nordibird, whose posts have been analyzed in detail in relation to the 'child-centric motherhood' discourse, MicrobatSister positions herself as a passive participant in relation to her child (her '8.5 yr old DS' in particular), and shows a willingness to put up with extreme boredom in order to meet his needs to 'talk about Minecraft for at least an hour' (lines 2-3) or 'natte[r] endlessly on and on and on' (line 6).

When the discourses of 'gendered parenthood', 'classed motherhood', 'commercialized motherhood' and 'child-centric motherhood' merge in this post, they work to position MicrobatSister as a gendered, classed subject who is entirely responsible for her children as 'products' and is positioned and evaluated in relation to these children. In other words, she is positioned, in line with persistent ideals and expectations in a contemporary western context, as a 'good mother'. This is not a position that contributors take up in any straightforward way; as noted earlier, the play and humour at the heart of 'Can we have a child exchange?' work to complicate this positioning and create an underlying tone of critique that will be further explored in Chapter 6.

There are two posts to 'Your identity as a mother' in which contributors make direct reference to the subject position of the 'good mother'. One of these posts, written by MrsPennyapple (Extract 5.9), draws together several discourses of gendered parenthood.

Extract 5.9 Post 66 from 'Your identity as a mother'

MrsPennyapple Wed 04-Jun-14 12:04:45

1. At the moment I am filled with the overwhelming sense that I
2. just don't matter. It doesn't matter if I come on my period and am

3. bleeding heavily and just want to take two minutes in the
4. bathroom by myself. It doesn't matter if something I want to hear
5. has come on the news. It doesn't matter if I've had a shit night's
6. sleep. I have tried to talk to DH about it but he just doesn't get it.
7. Last night he responded with 'but you're a good mum, and that's
8. what's important'. Just completely compounded and confirmed
9. everything I'm feeling. I am the least important person in my
10. own life.

When MrsPennyapple's husband invokes the 'good mum' category (line 7), which evaluates women in relation to their successful adoption of the subject position 'mum', he positions her within a discourse of 'child-centric motherhood'. By differentiating the parental roles of herself and her husband according to gender, MrsPennyapple also draws on the overarching discourse of 'gendered parenthood'. Whilst she presents herself as the parent who makes continual sacrifices for her children and is always *with* her children – for example by listing the personal sacrifices she makes for them (lines 2–6) – her statement 'he just doesn't get it' implies that her husband, by contrast, does not have the same personal and/or emotional investment in their children's lives. This opposition also works to position MrsPennyapple within the 'mother as main parent' discourse, as the parent who undertakes primary responsibility for their children. The convergence of these three discourses, 'child-centric motherhood', 'mother as main parent' and 'gendered parenthood', works to very powerfully position MrsPennyapple as a 'good mother' – as a primary carer who is completely devoted to and positioned in relation to her children.

The discussion of these examples in which several discourses of gendered parenthood merge to position Mumsnet users as 'good mothers' affirms claims across a range of sociological literature that the concept of 'good' mothering continues to be culturally tied to middle class values, child-centricity and essentialist notions of women's 'natural' predisposition towards caring, nurturing roles. This is despite claims that digital media, including forums such as Mumsnet Talk, can empower users to express themselves in multiple ways, and move beyond socio-cultural expectations and constraints (see Chapter 3). This analysis and discussion also show, importantly, that discourses of gendered parenthood often draw in and merge with other discourses, constituting specific ways in which women, as 'mothers', can be positioned in relation to children, in exclusively caring subject positions. Through such interdiscursivity, discourses of gendered parenthood ultimately become more powerful, because it becomes increasingly difficult to untangle the web of intersecting discourses that

merge to produce subject positions such as the 'good mother'. In the digital context of Mumsnet Talk, contributors are able to engage with and
negotiate these discourses, but they do not seem able to completely escape
them.

Resisting gendered parenthood

The discourses that have been outlined in this chapter so far are all gendered. The remaining discourses identified through analysis of Mumsnet
Talk – 'equal parenting' and 'individuality' – are arguably not gendered.
In this section, I introduce these discourses and show that they are often
positioned in competition with discourses of gendered parenthood, offering
non-gendered subject positions, such as 'parent' or 'me', in opposition to
gendered subject positions, such as 'mother'. 'Equal parenting' and 'individuality' therefore offer sites for the resistance and negotiation of gendered
parenthood in the Mumsnet Talk threads, especially 'Your identity as a
mother'. I also show, however, that the way contributors draw on discourses
of gendered parenthood in the constitution of these oppositional discourses
serves to amplify the profoundly gendered construction of parenthood in
Mumsnet Talk interactions.

Equal parenting

A discourse of 'equal parenting' can be seen to operate in the 'Your identity
as a mother' thread at moments where participants make a second parent
relevant to the interaction and position both themselves and this second
parent in a way that suggests they have equal parental roles. This discourse
is able to offer equal parental subject positions, regardless of gender, and
therefore compete with the 'mother as main parent', 'absent fathers', and
'child-centric motherhood' discourses.

The competing relation between 'equal parenting' and 'mother as main
parent'/'absent fathers' can be identified through close scrutiny of the
positioning of men within the 'Your identity as a mother' thread. In the
analysis presented in the previous section, I showed how the first-person
pronouns that dominate this thread mark the absence of fathers, excluding
men from parental subjectivities and positioning women as the main carers
for their children. I also showed how contributors such as MorningTimes
position themselves and their husbands as oppositional subjects. Within
the discourse of 'equal parenting', however, both parents tend to be made
relevant to the discussion, and positioned as part of an equal unit who act
jointly. For example, in post 11 (Extract 5.10), EggNChips uses inclusive
pronouns, such as 'we', 'us' and 'our', to present herself and her 'DP'
(darling partner) as a unit with equal parental roles. This simple difference

in pronoun choice brings EggNChips's partner into the family sphere and positions them both on a more equal footing (the potentially transformative function of shifts like this is noted at the start of Chapter 2).

Extract 5.10 Post 11 from 'Your identity as a mother'

EggNChips Sun 01-Jun-14 18:49:33

1. I was ready to become a mum when I had my DS [darling son],
2. it was well worth waiting for –we'd mellowed as a couple and
3. both completed our post grad courses/worked up to a good
4. place in employment and by the time he arrived, everything felt
5. right.

6. As soon as I became a mum, I was 100% mum and loved it;
7. threw myself in to just that. Then slowly over time, returning to
8. work initially part time, then more or less full time, I'm more
9. 'me'.

10. I'm of course a mum at home but DP [darling partner] does
11. equal amounts of parenting and between us we allow each other
12. to do our own things (so I play for a sports team, do stuff the
13. NCT [National Childbirth Trust], and regularly organize a meal
14. out with my girlfriends; he's training for a sport thing and also
15. meets his friend about an ongoing project). We also try and
16. have a date night or some time on our own once in a while. DS
17. has changed us, but only priorities, rather than us as people.

18. Now DS is 2.8, I'm 50% mum and 50% me, I love my job, love
19. my friends, love Dp, and my sports and there is so much more
20. to me than being a parent.

EggNChips's use of the preposition 'between [us]' in this post (line 11) also positions herself and her partner in close relation to one another. She also uses lexically and syntactically similar sentences to list the 'things' that they allow each other to do, in the clauses 'I play for a sports team' (line 12) / 'he's training for a sport thing' (line 14), and '[I] regularly organize a meal out with my girlfriends' (lines13-14) / '[He] meets his friend' (line 15). These twinned constructions imply that both parents take part in an equal range of activities outside of the home, and that their interests are very similar, therefore again positioning them as parents who share their time at home with their children. This analysis makes it apparent that a discourse of 'equal parenting' can intersect with a discourse of 'gendered parenthood' in Mumsnet Talk interactions: male and female parents can take up different subject positions, as 'mothers' and 'fathers', yet it is possible to construct (or at least attempt to construct) these subject positions as equal.

Despite the implication of parental equality in EggNChips's post, however, she can still be seen to take up the 'mother as main parent' discourse here. For example, in the statement 'DP [darling partner] does equal amounts of parenting' (lines 10-11), EggNChips subtly positions herself as the parent with primary responsibility, whose contribution is automatically assumed, and the standard by which her partner's parenting contribution is compared. In addition, she positions herself within a discourse of 'gendered parenthood', as a 'mum', in the first line of each paragraph of her post. Her use of the qualifier '100%' in line 6, further, positions her as a 'child-centric' mother, who is positioned exclusively in relation to her child. In line 10, the pre-clause qualifier 'of course' implies that her position as 'mum' in the home environment has 'common-sense' status. By contrast, she does not position her partner directly as a father or as a parent; he is described as someone who 'does . . . parenting' (lines 10-11). Whereas EggNChips repeatedly positions herself in a gendered parental role, then, her positioning of her DP is in many ways *not* equal; as in MorningTimes's post, which is analyzed earlier in relation to the 'mother as main parent' and 'absent fathers' discourses, this male subject is described, instead, in relation to the things he *does*. Whilst the 'equal parenting' discourse offers the potential for equality between parents, this interaction therefore shows that the *in*equality of 'common-sense' ideas about mothers and fathers makes it difficult to enact or express this equality in practice.

As well as offering 'equal' subject positions for mothers and fathers, the 'equal parenting' discourse can also offer a gender-neutral subject position, 'parent', which can compete with the gendered subject positions of 'mother' and 'father'. Whilst the categories 'mother' and 'father' relate to distinct gendered subject positions, 'parent' offers the same subject position, regardless of gender. NotCitrus takes up this gender-neutral subject position in post 13 of 'Your identity as a mother', which is reproduced in Extract 5.11 (see bold highlights).

Extract 5.11 Post 13 from 'Your identity as a mother'

NotCitrus Sun 01-Jun-14 19:26:59

1. **Parent** is a strong part of my identity, but far from the whole of
2. it even when it's seemed parenting is what occupies all of my
3. time. I felt so much more balanced a few months ago when I
4. managed my first night away from dc2 [second darling child],

5. even though since then the children have had to occupy most of
6. my energy.

7. I feel much more of a **parent** than a 'mum', even when I was
8. breastfeeding (nearly 4 years over 2 kids) – I didn't feel anything
9. female-specific since they stopped smelling of my insides.

10. Even with PND [postnatal depression] and stress and pain I
11. never regretted having them, which I think is down to being
12. older and spending years trying to conceive, so I knew I really
13. wanted them.

NotCitrus's use of the 'parent' category is unusual within the thread as a whole and therefore constitutes a marked choice, especially in her opening statement 'parent is a strong part of my identity'. This direct response to the question posed at the start of the thread, 'how much of your identity is bound up with being a mum?', rejects the 'mum' category that pandarific offers. NotCitrus is also the only user of the 'parent' category who explicitly justifies this choice (implying that it's quite a deliberate one), which she does with reference to gender between lines 8 and 9. Here, she implies that the gendering of parental subjectivity is unnecessary, or irrelevant to her, and therefore both highlights and contests the common-sense legitimacy of 'gendered parenthood'. She also suggests that the subject position 'parent' is mutually exclusive to the subject position 'mum' when she compares them in line 7.

Despite the fact that she takes up the gender-neutral subject position 'parent', however, both the overarching discourse of 'gendered parenthood' and the more specific discourses of 'child-centric motherhood' and 'mother as main parent' underpin NotCitrus's words. For example, her use of singular pronouns to position herself in relation to her children throughout this post, including 'my' and 'I', works to create the impression that she is the only parent involved in her children's lives (it is not clear whether this is the case from the content of her post, and as noted in Chapter 3, I did not have access to additional information that might clarify this point). Her reference to 'breastfeeding' (line 8) and 'smelling of my insides' (line 9) further draws attention to the aspects of parenthood that are biologically gender-specific, as in cakesonatrain's post (see earlier). The 'absent fathers' and 'mother as main parent' discourses merge in this context, working to position NotCitrus as the 'main', or 'default', parent, and excluding male (or any other) carers from this subject position. Further, the 'child-centric motherhood' discourse is evident in her statement 'since then the children have had to occupy most of my energy' (lines 5-6), which implies that she is consumed by her parental role, giving most of herself to her children. NotCitrus also reinforces her love for, and devotion to, her children in the statements 'I never regretted having them' (lines 10-11) and 'I knew I really wanted them' (lines 12-13), emphasizing her commitment with the adverbial qualifiers 'never' and 'really'. The way the 'absent fathers', 'mother as main parent' and 'child-centric motherhood' discourses merge and interrelate in this post works very powerfully to position NotCitrus as a mum who is child-centred and has primary responsibility for her children, despite her avoidance of the gendered subject position 'mum' itself. This demonstrates, again, that gendered parental roles are difficult for Mumsnet users to escape, underpinning even constructions of parenthood that can seem, on the surface, to be gender-neutral.

Individuality

'Individuality' is the second discourse that competes with discourses of gendered parenthood in the 'Your identity as a mother' thread. The following excerpts show that, just as the discourses of 'gendered parenthood' and 'child-centric motherhood' are realized most persistently through participants' self-identification as 'mums' in 'Your identity as a mother', a discourse of 'individuality' is repeatedly made apparent through double reference to self within variants of the clause 'I am me', where a first-person pronoun takes both the grammatical subject and complement positions. These claims are made particularly emphatically in posts 14 and 44, where the clause stands as a complete sentence, and in post 72, where the participant uses the intensifier 'totally' to make her claim that she is 'completely' herself explicit, in the same way that the author of post 11 claimed that she was '100% mum' (see earlier analysis of 'child-centric motherhood').

> Post 12. *IdealistAndProudOfIt*. I am me as I have always been
> Post 14. *Casmama*. I am me.
> Post 44. *catsrus*. I am who I am.
> Post 72. *museumum*. I am totally me.. the same me as before..

Because a discourse of 'individuality' positions subjects as individuals, not as members of a generic category, it can be taken up as a way of actively opposing being positioned as a particular 'type' of person. In 'Your identity as a mother', it tends to be taken up as a way of resisting being positioned as a 'mother', especially a 'child-centric mother'. Such opposition between 'individuality' and 'child-centric motherhood' is particularly apparent in posts such as Crazym's (Extract 5.12), where contributors take up a position as an individual as part of their resistance to being categorized as a mum.

Extract 5.12 Post 13 to 'Your identity as a mother'

Crazym Sun 01-Jun-14 19:07:32

1. Hate being identified as 'mum'.
2. I was a person before I became a mum and that person
3. still exists. being a mum is just a part of who I am, not the whole.
4. Used to hate the silly bint at nursery who, when I went to collect
5. the Dcs [darling children] would say 'and how are you today,
6. mum?'
7. I have a name!!!! I am a person!!

In this post, Crazym resists being positioned exclusively as 'mum' in favour of a more individualistic subject position – the 'I' introduced in line 2. The opening and closing statements of her post capture her emphatic resistance by presenting the subject positions 'mum' and 'I' as oppositional: 'Hate being identified as "mum" . . . I am a person!!'. Her use of six exclamation marks in two unmitigated four-word sentences in line 7, furthermore, suggest that she is fighting to express her individuality; that she actively opposes being positioned as a 'mum', at least by others who are not her children. It is worth pointing out that Crazym does actually position *herself* as a 'mum' in this post through the relational processes 'became a mum. . . / being a mum' in lines 2-3. This shows, as with the analysis of 'child-centric motherhood', that a discourse of 'gendered parenthood' can intersect with other discourses: Crazym is able to position herself as both a mum *and* an individual. Her statement 'a part of who I am, not the whole' (line 3) clarifies Crazym's *partial* identification with the subject position 'mum'. The 'child-centric motherhood' discourse, however, works to position subjects as mothers to the exclusion of all other subject positions. It seems to be this position as a 'total', 'child-centric' mother that Crazym works to resist. As shown earlier, she does so by presenting the subject positions 'mum' and 'I' as oppositional, and through emphatic emphasis of her self-positioning as the latter – as an 'individual'. She also evaluates being identified as a 'mum' in negative terms, through both the opening evaluation 'hate' and her negative evaluation of the nursery worker who calls her 'mum' as a 'silly bint' (line 4), a highly derogatory term that points to Crazym's anger and frustration – channelled, at this moment, in the direction of this woman.[4]

The opposition between 'individuality' and 'child-centric motherhood' is also evident at several other moments in the 'Your identity as a mother' thread. For example, in the post by MrsPennyapple that was explored earlier (Extract 5.9), converging discourses of gendered parenthood work to position MrsPennyapple as a 'good mother', who is completely devoted to her children. However, the closing statement of MrsPennyapple's post, 'I am the least important person in my own life', crystallizes the tone of resentment and frustration that pervades her post. Here, MrsPennyapple positions herself as an individual through her use of the personal pronoun 'I' and the double possessive '*my own* life'. This double emphasis on self draws attention to the paradox of her final statement, which implies that this self is suppressed; made irrelevant by her positioning as a good, 'child-centric' mother, whose *children* are the most important people in her life and define who she is. By positioning herself as an individual, or at least highlighting her inability to position herself as such, MrsPennyapple draws on a discourse of 'individuality' in order to convey her disapproval and dissatisfaction with being positioned as a 'child-centric mother', just as Crazym does in post 13 (further examples of the interplay between 'individuality' and 'child-centric motherhood' are offered in Mackenzie, 2018). My analysis of both posts again points to the pervasiveness of discourses of gendered parenthood, which have the binary gendered categories of mother and father at their core, as well as emphasizing the difficulty Mumsnet users have in escaping these discourses.

Concluding remarks

This chapter has shown that discourses of gendered parenthood are dominant and pervasive in the Mumsnet Talk threads that are analyzed here, persistently working to position Mumsnet users in restrictive gendered subject positions. It has drawn attention to some of the ways in which these discourses are reproduced through linguistic forms such as categories, pronouns and evaluations, captured in statements such as 'you're a good mum'. I have also shown that contributors may take up the subject positions that are offered by these discourses more indirectly – for example through indexical resources.

This chapter is significant both for social scientists interested in gender, parenthood and identity and for discourse studies scholars, because it names eight specific discourses that are taken up by Mumsnet users, which can be further explored in a range of contexts. I have suggested that the overarching discourse of 'gendered parenthood' binds together all of these discourses, inscribing a dichotomous gender divide between male and female parents that allows further, more specific and restrictive discourses to arise. The implications of these findings go beyond the academic context. As long as discourses of gendered parenthood continue to represent 'common-sense' meanings around gender, parenthood and raising children, the subject positions available to parents will be limited. It will be difficult for male parents, for example, to position themselves as 'main parents', and difficult for female parents to position themselves in a way that is not related to their children. Further, it is likely to be difficult for families who fall outside of the binary parental unit of mother and father, such as single, same-sex, non-binary or kinship carers and parents, to be valued and legitimized in a wider social context.

However, this chapter has also shown that contributors to 'Your identity as a mother' and 'Can we have a child exchange?' take up discourses that do not rely on gender differentiation, and that some of these discourses – namely 'equal parenting' and 'individuality' – often compete with discourses of gendered parenthood, such as 'mother as main parent' and 'child-centric motherhood'. Furthermore, contributors to these threads can be seen to resist and negotiate discourses of gendered parenthood in varied and multiple ways. The next chapter will explore some of the ways in which these negotiations are played out in Mumsnet Talk. This focus will reveal further insights for research in the areas of both discourse studies and gender and parenthood, across the social sciences. It will be particularly relevant for *digital* discourse studies, because it will show how digital, discursive and social frameworks intersect in Mumsnet Talk interactions.

Notes

1 The eight discourses that are presented in this chapter are first introduced in Mackenzie (2017a), which focuses on analysis of the 'Can we have a child exchange?' thread, and explores the discourses of 'gendered parenthood', 'child-centric motherhood', 'commercialized motherhood' (previously named 'commercialization') and 'classed motherhood', and Mackenzie (2018), which presents analysis of the 'Your identity as a mother' thread, and introduces 'mother as main parent', 'absent fathers', 'equal parenting' and 'individuality'. In this chapter I draw on, elaborate and bring together the analyses and insights that were first presented in these publications. Aspects of these articles are reproduced with the permission of SAGE Publications (Mackenzie, 2017a) and Equinox Publishing Ltd (Mackenzie, 2018).
2 As noted in Chapter 4, all extracts from Mumsnet Talk are reproduced with the permission of both the individual authors of the posts and Mumsnet Limited. The majority of usernames are reproduced as in the original posts, but some are pseudonyms, at participants' requests.

3 Here and throughout this book, acronyms in Mumsnet users' posts are glossed in square brackets.

4 It is interesting that Crazym uses the derogatory gendered term 'bint' to position this female nursery worker, considering her own rejection of this person's use of the gendered 'mum' (which does not have the same explicitly negative connotations). When I contacted her to ask for consent, Crazym expressed regret at using the word 'bint', suggesting that she was aware of the potential irony in her choice of words.

6 Negotiating, resisting and subverting discourses of gendered parenthood in Mumsnet Talk[1]

In Chapter 5, I showed that Mumsnet Talk users take up a range of discourses that work to position themselves, and others, in specific gendered subject positions: for example as 'mums', and sometimes 'good mums', who are often 'child-centred' and the 'main parent' to their children. The presence of these discourses has been illustrated with reference to linguistic patterns and practices, such as referential devices and resources that are indexically linked to social categories, such as gender and class. I also pointed to some moments at which Mumsnet users express their frustration or dissatisfaction with restrictive parental subject positions, and use strategies that work to complicate or subvert these positions. This chapter focuses on some of these 'significant moments' (as defined in Chapter 4) in more detail. It presents an in-depth exploration of some of the resources and strategies Mumsnet users deploy in order to negotiate and position themselves in relation to dominant discourses of gendered parenthood at these moments, with a particular focus on double-voicing, evaluation, alignment and play. This linguistic analysis is underpinned by a feminist poststructuralist perspective, which supports nuanced consideration of the multiple and potentially competing ways in which Mumsnet Talk users may be positioned at any one moment, and subsequent discussion of both the dominant norms and transformative practices that are at work in their interactions. This approach distinguishes the Mumsnet study from previous literature on gender and parenthood, and reveals key insights about how women who are parents negotiate their identities in relation to wider discursive forces in a popular online parenting discussion forum.

Negotiating child-centric motherhood in 'Your identity as a mother': double-voicing, evaluation and alignment

Contributors to both 'Your identity as a mother' and 'Can we have a child exchange?' often draw on the words or presumed thoughts of other people. This representation of others often involves evaluation and alignment, as contributors position themselves in relation to those others, as either positively aligned, negatively aligned or at some point between the two. In this section, I explore the ways in which Mumsnet users draw on alignment and evaluation to position themselves in relation to discourses of gendered parenthood in an interactional sequence from 'Your identity as a mother'. This exploration draws on theories of positioning (Davies and Harré, 1990), double-voicing (Baxter, 2014), evaluation and alignment (Du Bois, 2007), as defined in Chapter 4. The sequence that will be analyzed here is identified as a 'significant moment' because it is a site of contested knowledge, power and subjectivity where contributors negotiate discourses of gendered parenthood, especially 'child-centric motherhood', through a discussion about 'attachment parents'.[2]

The catalyst for the interactional sequence that is explored here comes in post 37. This post was written by an anonymous author who introduces the category 'attachment parent' with reference to a colleague who, she suggests, uses the label to make an exaggerated statement about 'who she is'.[3] Subsequent posts, which are reproduced in Extract 6.1, respond to post 37, to each other, and address the overall theme of the thread, with a focus on how parental subjectivity can be defined in relation to schools of thought such as 'attachment parenting'. The parenting philosophy at the heart of this interaction is based on the theories of attachment that were developed by psychologists Bowlby and Ainsworth (Ainsworth and Bowlby, 1991; Bowlby, 1969), with the term 'attachment parenting' later being coined and promoted to a wider audience by Sears and Sears (2003). This philosophy is very relevant to the 'child-centric motherhood' discourse because it demands a high level of parental commitment and devotion (it is primarily *mothers* who are addressed in this and related literature on attachment parenting). It promotes close and continual emotional attachment and physical connection between parents and their babies or infants that would potentially make it difficult to engage with other activities, roles and relationships in the early years of a child's life. Through the interactional sequence that is presented ahead, several contributors to 'Your identity as a mother' jointly construct and negotiate the defining characteristics of the group who adopt this parenting philosophy, who are variously labelled as 'attachment parents', 'AP mums', and 'the "if you have any time for yourself you're neglectful" brigade'. I suggest ahead that, in the space of this interaction, this hypothetical 'attachment parenting' group becomes the voice of the 'child-centric motherhood' discourse. They are presented as powerful and dominant at times, but this power, the value of the knowledge they are said to impart about motherhood and the validity of their positioning of themselves and others as 'child-centric' mothers, is contested in multiple ways.

*Extract 6.1 Attachment parenting: an interactional sequence
from 'Your identity as a mother'*[3]

39. Thurlow Tue 03-Jun-14 16:04:35

1. That does make sense, **username removed***. I don't know
2. anyone like that in RL [real life] but I do occasionally come
3. across posters on MN [Mumsnet] whose comments can make me
4. think what you think. It is a sense of deciding on and then
5. clinging to an identity as an attachment parent, unconditional
6. parent etc.

7. In other circumstances I would wonder whether someone who
8. decided so deliberately to define themselves but one
9. characteristic or belief was unsure of themselves, but I don't
10. know whether that would apply to mothers.

11. I suspect – crap cod-psychology here – that for some people
12. who deliberately define themselves but something such as, for
13. example, attachment parenting, they are doing it as an extreme
14. way of explaining or confirming their decisions. That might be
15. completely wrong but sometimes it is the impression I get – I
16. am right, I AM!

*author of post 37

56. Dysfunctional Tue 03-Jun-14 21:53:34

1. **pandarific-** May I ask what fiction you have been reading?
2. Interesting topic and I am someone who practiced 'attachment
3. parenting' much derided above. Why did I do it? Because I was
4. doing all those things associated with attachment parenting and
5. then heard the label and rather liked the fact that I could parent
6. that intensely as it suited my obsessive nature. I read everything
7. there was to read about parenting to make sure I was doing it
8. right.

9. My life revolved around the DC [darling children] and my
10. identity disappeared (It's starting to recover after almost 7
11. years).

12. I envy those to whom it seems to come naturally and easily.

59. Viglioso Wed 04-Jun-14 08:26:39

1. [tagged quote from post 37 – removed]

2. This is very interesting as an older pregnant woman (through
3. medical necessity not choice, which might have a bearing on my
4. own perceptions) who is one of the last of her peers to have a
5. DC.

6. I almost notice from the 'outside' looking in that some *do* have a
7. certain way – e.g. a book/movement/lifestyle – of parenting that
8. they define themselves by: but it's almost like being part of a
9. tribe, rather than inherently to do with being a mum IYSWIM [if
10. you see what I mean]? Lots of judgement and looking at the
11. way other people do things and defining by the binary opposite.

12. Can you guess some have been a PITA [pain in the arse]
13. already lecturing me (good mums don't, apparently, wear make-
14. up: that money/time could be spent on PFB [precious first-
15. born]).

16. Interestingly one of the most devoted mum in terms of practical
17. things and passionate adoration of PFB I know (of child with a
18. disability requiring lots of care and special input) is very much
19. – and vocally – her 'own woman' *with* her child by her side
20. IYSWIM.

21. I'm actually a bit terrified of the 'if you have any time for
22. yourself you're neglectful' brigade. As I mentioned above, if
23. anything I'll end up accidentally attached or just spoil PFB due
24. to PFB being a bit of a miracle . . . but I would like to
25. be *allowed* to be me. ☺

60. Thurlow Wed 04-Jun-14 10:02:24

1. **Dysfunctional** – I'm sorry, I didn't mean to sound as if I was
2. deriding attachment parenting. I was using it as an example;
3. currently I am more aware of parents who follow attachment
4. parenting who have it as an entire ethos of their life, but I don't
5. mean to suggest it is the attachment parenting itself which is bad.
6. Whatever works for you and your baby ☺ It just seems to be
7. the current outrider for a parenting style/theory that is very
8. strongly embraced and used to define most of what a parent

9. does. A decade or two ago it would probably have been GF
10. [Gina Ford – childcare expert and author].
*
∴ . .
*second part of post omitted; strays from topic of sequence.

80. Dysfunctional Wed 04-Jun-14 19:47:40

1. **Thurlow** no offence taken. I know what you mean by the AP
2. [attachment parenting] 'tribe'. I never felt a part of that as I
3. worked part time and the local AP 'mums' (proving that I am as
4. guilty as anyone of identifying people purely by the
5. characteristic that they've given birth) I knew were all white
6. middle class SAHMs [stay-at-home mums] who didn't seem to
7. mix much outside their tribe and frequented singing groups and
8. created their own toddler group.

9. I used to go to my local children's centre in the poorer area of the
10. city where I lived and there was much more of a mix of ages,
11. cultures and classes. We were of course brought together by the
12. fact that we had DC though so in that way we did have to first
13. identify as mums to find common ground

The 'child-centric motherhood' discourse is repeatedly taken up, negotiated and resisted throughout the sequence presented in Extract 6.1. In post 56, for example, Dysfunctional's claim that, as an attachment parent, 'my life revolved around the DC and my identity disappeared' (lines 9-10) both suggests that her relation to her children had total influence over her sense of self and positions her own needs as secondary to her children's. Dysfunctional's use of the verbs 'revolved' and 'disappeared' positions children at the centre of her life. They also imply that her 'life' and 'identity' are entities over which she has no control. This statement suggests that Dysfunctional's subjectivity is defined by a discourse that positions her exclusively in relation to her children, as a 'child-centric mother'.

The way the 'child-centric motherhood' discourse can work to fix female subjects in imperative and powerless positions is made further apparent in post 59, where Viglioso reproduces this discourse quite explicitly through the imagined voice of attachment parents, in the statements 'good mums don't, apparently, wear make-up: that money/time could be spent on PFB' (lines 13-14) and 'if you have any time for yourself you're neglectful' (lines 21-22). These are both examples of dialogic double-voicing, whereby ideas are debated 'as if the speaker is both the addresser and the addressee' (Baxter, 2014: 5; see explanation of double-voicing in Chapter 4). Both of the constructions in these excerpts work to directly position women in relation to their children, as either 'good' or 'neglectful' mums, according to certain criteria. At this moment, Viglioso is able to contest the legitimacy of the 'child-centric motherhood' discourse by reproducing it through the voice of attachment parents. Her use of this strategy echoes Jensen's (2013) example of a thread where Mumsnet users engaged in imagined dialogue with caricatures of 'perfect' mothers (see Chapter 3). In both Jensen's data and the 'Your identity as a mother' thread, contributors can be seen to 'defensively ward off' particular types of 'good' mothers (Jensen, 2013: 142).

Contributors to this interactional sequence further contest the legitimacy of the 'child-centric motherhood' discourse through negative evaluations of the attachment parenting group. For example, in post 60, Thurlow implies that attachment parents have an unreasonable and extreme commitment to a particular ethos of parenting through her use of superlative and intensifying language to describe this commitment, as in the phrases 'entire ethos' (line 4) and 'very strongly embraced' (lines 7-8). Viglioso negatively evaluates the group in even more explicit terms in post 59, with her use of the negative descriptor 'PITA' (pain in the arse) (line 12). Further, the overbearing tone that she attributes to the reported speech of attachment parents, in the statement 'good mums don't . . . wear make-up' (lines 13-14), and her use of the verb 'lecturing' (line 13) to frame this reported speech, implies that they are unreasonable, domineering, and have an overinflated sense of their own importance. Through their persistently negative evaluations of these 'others', both Thurlow and Viglioso negatively align with attachment parents and their values, and thus distance themselves from and contest the 'child-centric motherhood' discourse that attachment parents come to represent in this sequence. By focusing on an imagined group who voices this discourse, they make a somewhat abstract force personal and tangible: it is difficult to contest dominant discourses, but that resistance is made possible here through imagined debate with, and disparagement of, a relatively specific group.

As well as dialogic double-voicing, which principally works to ward off threats (as explained in Chapter 4), there are also many examples of interaction that are oriented towards *positive* alignment with others in this sequence. Such alignment is achieved through a linguistic strategy variously called 'dialogic syntax' (Du Bois, 2014: 359) or 'matching and mirroring' (Coates, 1996: 203), whereby individuals echo the words or structures of one another's utterances (also see Tannen, 2007, on repetition and interpersonal involvement). This kind of repetition in interaction is closely related to the concept of double-voicing, but it does not result in the same engagement with the concerns of another, or orientation towards another 'voice'. Rather, it creates the effect that several interlocutors are using *one* voice, or as Tannen (2007: 62) puts it, 'a shared universe of discourse'. For example, Dysfunctional (post 80, line 2) repeats Viglioso's (post 59, line 9) use of the label 'tribe' to negatively evaluate attachment parents as a group. Viglioso also uses the similar category 'brigade' (line 22), which, like 'tribe', has connotations of combat and hostility. In addition, both Thurlow (post 39) and Viglioso (post 59) use generic, impersonal referential devices, such as 'some' (Viglioso, lines 6 and 12), 'someone' (Thurlow, line 7) and 'some people' (Thurlow, line 11), which work to position attachment parents as a group of nameless, anonymous 'others'. They also both imply that this group of people force themselves into a false identity by referring to their attempts to 'define themselves' (line 8 in both posts) in particular ways. The way these contributors echo one another's words and constructions works both to create a sense of shared disapproval towards 'attachment parents' and to create positive alignment, solidarity and a sense of in-group membership between one another. This collaboration and mutual alignment through repetition is a key resource in their negotiation of the 'child-centric motherhood' discourse, because they reinforce the distance between themselves as an 'in-group' and the others who voice the 'child-centric motherhood' discourse as an 'out-group'.

Further, Thurlow and Viglioso use a range of mitigating devices to invite a wider group of readers to collaborate in the joint construction of, and negative alignment with, the 'attachment parenting' group. For example, Thurlow (post 39) uses speculative verbs such as 'wonder' (line 7), 'suspect' (line 11) and 'don't know' (lines 9-10), modals such as 'would' (line 7) and 'might' (line 14) and adverbs such as 'sometimes' (line 15) to frame her constructions as hypothetical and uncertain. Viglioso (post 59) uses similar mitigating devices, such as the discourse marker 'IYSWIM' (if you see what I mean) (lines 9 and 20) and adverbs such as 'almost' (lines 6 and 8) and 'actually' (line 21) to frame her construction of this group as provisional – dependent on the acquiescence of her readers. This collaborative style further adds to the sense that contributors are part of an in-group, working together in the construction of an out-group who represent 'child-centric motherhood', and collectively disapproving this discourse.

Contributors to this sequence also position both themselves and each other as part of a wider in-group of Mumsnet users by assuming shared understanding of specialist terms, such as 'attachment parent' and 'unconditional parent', and by employing resources that are common throughout this discussion forum, such as those listed in Figure 6.1. By employing these specialist resources, contributors are able to affirm their in-group membership and create a sense of affinity and togetherness with other Mumsnet users. Elsewhere (Mackenzie, 2017b: 306), I have explored how such shared practices, both on the larger scale of practices across the whole forum and on a smaller scale in relation to more ephemeral in-groups such as the one explored earlier, can also work to target a specific audience of Mumsnet users, and potentially make it difficult for readers who are not so familiar with the site to access meaning, thus adding a 'layer of privacy' to Mumsnet interactions.

The use of shared, in-group resources in the 'Your identity as a mother' thread, however, may also limit the ways in which contributors are able to express themselves. For example, their use of 'darling' acronyms, the

---

- 'tagging' other users: 'That does make sense, **username removed**';
- acronyms: 'MN' [Mumsnet], 'DC' [darling child(ren)], 'PFB' [precious first-born];
- emojis: '☺'
- strikethrough text: '~~or just spoil PFB~~'.

Figure 6.1 Digital resources in the 'attachment parenting' sequence

most popular of which include 'DC' (darling child/ children), 'DH' (darling husband) and 'DP' (darling partner), has become a widely accepted shorthand for 'child(ren)', 'husband' or 'partner' within Mumsnet Talk. Through these acronyms, the positioning of children, husbands and partners in an exclusively positive way is taken for granted, and can even be seen as compulsory, within this space. Where it is children who are being labelled 'darling', these positive evaluations work to position contributors as proud, loving parents who celebrate and admire their children: in other words, as child-centric mothers. The positioning of husbands and (male) partners as 'darling' may be seen as part of a broader potential discourse of 'family-centric motherhood', which positions the 'nuclear', heterosexual family of a father, mother and children as an unbreakable, loving unit, with the mother at its centre. Of course, there are many moments at which the use of 'darling' acronyms could be read as ironic, especially considering the frequently humorous and subversive nature of Mumsnet Talk interactions. Nevertheless, the pervasiveness of the 'darling' acronyms can be seen as one of the ways in which common practices within the Mumsnet Talk forum work not only to facilitate Mumsnet users' negotiation of dominant discourses of gendered parenthood but also to constrain their access to a range of discursive positions, making it difficult for them to escape forms of knowledge that position family relations as exclusively loving bonds.

The analysis and discussion of the following section further explore the ways in which collective alignment can be a powerful force for negotiating dominant discourses of gendered parenthood in Mumsnet Talk, yet can also work to restrict the forms of expression available to members of this forum.

Negotiating gendered parenthood in 'Can we have a child exchange?': play and collective alignment

It is suggested in Chapter 3 that the affordances of many digital contexts, such as anonymity and related opportunities for play, may facilitate individuals' negotiation and resistance of dominant sociocultural norms, expectations and constraints. This section considers the transgressive potential of play and humour in particular, which are persistent features of both the threads that are analyzed in this book, and the forum more widely. I focus on the 'Can we have a child exchange?' thread, which is particularly reliant on humour and play, showing how contributors deploy these strategies to negotiate and subvert discourses of gendered parenthood. The analysis that is presented here continues to draw on theories of positioning (Davies and Harré, 1990) and double-voicing (Baxter, 2014), which were introduced in Chapter 4.

The 'Can we have a child exchange?' thread relies on a good deal of collaboration between users as they collectively key the classified advertisement frame (the nature of which is detailed in Chapter 5). The linguistic conventions they employ in order to do so are evident in the excerpts presented in Extract 6.2.

Extract 6.2 Keying the classified advertisement frame: posts 1, 4, 37 and 52 from 'Can we have a child exchange?'

1. BertieBotts Wed 16-Jul-14 13:23:30

1. I can offer one (currently) sweaty and exuberant 5 year old.
2. Reads most things. Speaks some German. Quite helpful around
3. the house.

4. Reason for sale: Excessive farting.

5. Any takers? 😬

4. ChaosTrulyReigns Wed 16-Jul-14 13:32:29

1. I've got am extremely useful 11yi DD [11-year-old darling daughter].
2. Reason for swap? 3 gazillion wayward loom bands that she **needs** inhher
3. possession at all times.

4. Please may have the socksorter?

5. Chars.

37. Wilberforce2 Wed 16-Jul-14 15:01:52

1. I can offer a lovely 4.5 month old baby girl who is getting desperate to
2. eat and will attack you for food and drink! I don't mind having her back
3. when she is fully weaned 😊

4. In return I can take any child that will give me a full nights sleep!

52. Clobbered Wed 16-Jul-14 20:49:07

1. Model 1: Twenty-one, driver, non-smoker, recent graduate. Self-caring
2. but tendency to wake early and pace the floor.

3. Model 2: Twenty, excellent cook and percussionist. Extreme clothing
4. abuse (floordrobe currently occupying 2 rooms of the house).

5. Model 3: Screen-bound thirteen year old. Obsessed with Lego and
6. Geomag. Likes cats but couldn't eat a whole one.

7. Free to good home.

Most of these excerpts begin with a ritualistic opening, whereby the 'object for sale' is introduced with a pronoun-verb 'offer' phrase, followed by an extended noun phrase, as in the opening statements 'I've got am extremely useful 11yi DD' (post 4, line 1) and 'I can offer a lovely 4.5 month old baby girl who is getting desperate to eat' (post 37, lines 1-2). As noted in the exploration of 'commercialized motherhood' in Chapter 5, contributors to this thread tend to use an indefinite article or numeral such as 'a', 'an' or 'one' to introduce these noun phrases, further working to position their children as commodities, or objects for sale. These ritualistic openings may include, or be immediately followed by, extended descriptions and evaluations of the children in question, sometimes in the form of elliptical lists of their qualities, as in BertieBotts's description 'Reads most things. Speaks some German. Quite helpful around the house' (post 1, lines 2-3) and Clobbered's 'Twenty-one, driver, non-smoker, recent graduate' (post 52, line 1). In these posts, contributors often adopt similar evaluative modifiers to describe their children, such as the affective adjective 'lovely', which is used nine times across the thread by eight different participants, and 'cute', which is used five times by five different participants. Finally, posts tend to end with a ritualistic close, which alludes to the transaction process through an idiomatic or 'stock' phrase, as in the closing statements 'Reason for sale: Excessive farting. Any takers?' (post 1, lines 4-5) and 'Free to a good home' (post 52, line 8).

Participants' shared keying of the classified advertisement frame is central to the playful quality of 'Can we have a child exchange?'. By taking on the conventions of classified advertisements, contributors to this thread present their children as commodities of no particular consequence, which are freely available for sale or exchange. Yet, as noted in Chapter 5, contributors' posts are not likely to be mistaken for genuine pleas to exchange their children. Rather, through their play with well-known conventions, they create a prevailing sense that what is said is not necessarily what is meant (Bateson, 1972) – that this is an ostensibly non-serious thread, in which participants experiment with what can and cannot be said about children, and their own position in relation to those children. The effect of this play with words and social norms is humorous; posts to this thread are generally funny and witty, and presumably designed to be so. This strategy also creates a tone of irony and critique that allows contributors to position themselves in multiple ways. The nature of this complex discursive positioning is explored ahead.

Contributors to the 'Can we have a child exchange?' thread can be seen to position themselves, on one level, as female, middle class parents, who are entirely responsible and accountable for the 'value' of their children as commodities. This self-positioning, as explained in Chapter 5, relies on an interplay between several discourses of gendered parenthood, and converges to create the overall impression that they are 'good mothers'. However, the playful, humorous and ironic tone of the thread also works to subvert the values associated with these subject positions. For example, contributors apparently position themselves as 'middle class mothers' who deploy a wealth of cultural and economic resources to support their children's development and future success. Yet, on another level, their words can be read as an exaggerated performance of middle class motherhood, and thereby to mock their apparent desire to emphasize their children's expensive, time-consuming and intellectual pursuits. Contributors also employ an affectively oriented style that can be said to position them as female parents, drawing on the indexical ties between femininity, motherhood and love, affection and care for children. However, their words can also be interpreted as a playful parody of feminine motherhood, or a critique of the expectation that mothers should behave in a stereotypically 'feminine' way.

By positioning themselves as 'good mothers' in a playful and parodic context, contributors to 'Can we have a child exchange?' draw attention to and thereby critique the lines in the sand through which 'good motherhood' is drawn and the demands that are placed upon them as 'good mothers': to be 'feminine' and 'middle class', to be responsible for the 'value' of their children as commodities, and ultimately, to be positioned and evaluated in relation to their children. This resistance and challenge are all the more powerful because they are collaboratively constructed. Participants' shared use of formulaic words and structures in this thread means that they are able to both take up and negotiate dominant discourses of gendered parenthood as a *collective* voice that works together in the construction of meaning, rather than as many separate, individual voices. There are parallels here with Jaworska's (2017) analysis of Mumsnet Talk threads about postnatal depression (see Chapter 3), where she shows that the narrative practices of small confessions and exemplums make resistance and transformation of the 'good mother' possible. In 'Can we have a child exchange?', the conventions employed by contributors come from a very different genre, but their shared adoption of conventionalized resources nevertheless opens up a space in which they can negotiate discourses of gendered parenthood within the relative security of an established, shared framework.

Some contributors to 'Can we have a child exchange?' explicitly draw attention to their dual self-positioning. For example, in posts 11 and 58 (Extract 6.3), RoseberryTopping and WhispersofWickedness use linguistic and digital resources that signal the multiple possible interpretations of their words.

*Extract 6.3 Excerpts from 'Can we have a child exchange?':
posts 11 and 58*

11. RoseberryTopping Wed 16-Jul-14 13:59:44

1. I've got a 4 year old boy that is a bit of a free spirit ☺ he doesn't enjoy
2. sitting still but if you like being outside and running around a lot then
3. he's the boy for you. He's also partial to cake and will sometimes share.

4. Also got a newborn boy up for offers. He doesn't do much at the moment
5. but he's lovely to snuggle and smells nice ☺

58. WhispersOfWickedness Wed 16-Jul-14 21:28:59

1. I will take a newborn during the day or a teenager who spends all day in
2. their room 😀 (the driving 21yo [year-old] sounds ideal, but looks like
3. someone's already bagged them) I have a ~~PITA~~ [pain in the arse] cheeky
4. 4 yo who NEEDS to go to school now, I'll have him back at the
5. beginning of September ☺ He likes crafts (covering every surface in
6. glitter and using copious amounts of prittstick and PVA glue), the park
7. and Frozen.

8. Also have a princess and horse obsessed nearly 3yo. She is very
9. emotionally complex, so good luck figuring her out 😀 Very bossy,
10. definitely the ruler of our household. She is VERY cute though ☺

In post 58, WhispersofWickedness marks the evaluative descriptions 'cheeky' and 'likes crafts', which can be interpreted in a relatively positive way, as euphemistic alternatives to what she really wants to say: that her son is a 'PITA' (pain in the arse) (line 3) and likes 'covering every surface in glitter and using copious amounts of prittstick and PVA glue' (lines 5-6). However, she does not completely avoid these negative evaluations. Instead, she hides them deliberately badly, using strikethrough text and brackets to mask them, and therefore suggest that they are dispreferred and subversive without completely erasing them. Similarly, in post 11, RoseberryTopping's euphemistic description of her son as a 'free spirit' avoids an explicitly negative evaluation of her child, allowing her to maintain his position as a valuable commodity, and her own position as a 'good mother'. But the winking emoji placed after this description marks it as part of a performance of the expected, or acceptable, behaviour of the 'good mother' subject. It suggests a shared knowingness and points to her confidence that others will read a secondary, unspoken meaning behind this phrase (e.g. that he is uncontrollable, difficult or 'badly' behaved). These examples of double-speak point to an underlying power struggle within the playful contributions of this thread. By drawing attention to 'accepted' and 'unaccepted' forms of expression, contributors such as WhispersofWickedness and RoseberryTopping highlight the difficulty for women, as parents, to escape discourses that work to position them as 'good mothers'. The implication follows that, as subjects positioned by these discourses, women are expected to describe their children in particular ways – for example to evaluate them in positive terms even where their behaviour can be interpreted as negative or destructive. Such double-speak, alongside the pervasive irony of the thread, further draws attention to the 'common-sense' legitimacy of the 'good mother' subject position, yet distances contributors from it, and works to subvert it.

I suggested in Chapter 3 that play can be a resource that allows individuals to move beyond socio-cultural expectations and constraints – that multiple realities may be made possible by play. This claim is borne out by the more in-depth discussion and analysis that is presented here, which shows that play in 'Can we have a child exchange?' allows contributors to take up, but at the same time to parody and critique, the 'good mother' subject position, because it creates multiple layers of meaning and an undertone of irony. I have also shown that the collaborative nature of this play draws contributors together, building a sense of in-group membership and solidarity that supports this parody and critique. However, the collaborative nature of this thread can also be said to impose constraints upon its contributors. Whilst on the one hand, 'Can we have a child exchange?' is powerful in terms of its humour, irony and underlying critique, on the other hand it allows little space for diverse voices to be heard, or for participants to adopt subject positions that completely escape, or offer an alternative to, the 'good mother'. Like other scholars who have explored the way individuals orient to gender norms in online interactions (Gong, 2016; Hall et al., 2012; Milani, 2013; see Chapter 3), I have therefore found that contributors to 'Can we have a child exchange?' adopt a set of converging subject positions that are very much in line with sociocultural expectations. The way they take up these subject positions can be seen to critique, but at the same time to legitimize, discourses of gendered parenthood, reinforcing dominant ideals that 'good' mothers are feminine, child-centred and middle class.

Discussion and concluding remarks: who is it possible to be in Mumsnet Talk?

Building on the findings presented in the previous chapter, which showed how discourses of gendered parenthood are taken up and reproduced through linguistic forms such as categories, pronouns and evaluations, this chapter has revealed some of the communicative strategies Mumsnet users deploy as they negotiate these discourses. For example, it has shown that contributors to 'Your identity as a mother' and 'Can we have a child exchange?' frequently position themselves in relation to discourses of gendered parenthood through evaluation and alignment with others. This chapter has also emphasized the importance of collaborative interaction as a discursive resource in these threads, showing how positive alignment with others can add force to users' construction of transformative and subversive discursive positions. At the same time, however, I have suggested that in-group alignment between Mumsnet users can also restrict contributors' access to different subject positions and their ability to adopt an individual voice. In this section, I explore the implications of the findings set out in both this and the previous chapter, with a particular focus on the question of how women are able to negotiate their parental identities in relation to wider discursive forces in the context of the Mumsnet Talk discussion forum.

The previous commentary on 'Can we have a child exchange?' suggests that humour and play can allow contributors to subvert discourses of gendered parenthood, and the subject position of the 'good mother', in a way that will be accepted and valued within the Mumsnet community. Contributors' ability to playfully key the conventions of an established genre (classified advertisements) in this thread is by no means unique to the digital context, or to parenting discussion forums specifically, but it may be that the flexibility and openness of the discussion forum thread format make space for these users to take up diverse linguistic practices and resources in innovative ways. This claim is supported by Jaworska's (2017) findings about the use of narrative practices in Mumsnet Talk threads on the topic of post-natal depression (see earlier and Chapter 3). Mumsnet users' ability to deploy established resources in innovative ways may also be facilitated, at least in part, by the potential for anonymity in this digital context, which allows them to joke about transgressive topics, such as giving away their children, without fear of reprisal in their personal lives. In addition, it is likely that Mumsnet users' shared sense of belonging and mutual understanding of the frequently humorous nature of posts to the forum allow them to engage in spontaneous, subversive humour and play with the knowledge that their words are unlikely to be misconstrued or taken too seriously. These findings support claims in the wider literature (see Chapter 3) that the potential for anonymity, play and community membership in digital contexts can all work to engender an openness to the negotiation and subversion of dominant socio-cultural norms.

Another important point that emerges from this chapter is that Mumsnet users' self-positioning in relation to discourses of gendered parenthood is often achieved jointly, through interaction and intersubjective alignment. For example, I have pointed to the way Mumsnet users deploy collaborative strategies, such as repeating words and structures from one another's posts, to position themselves as members of an in-group who work together in the construction of meaning. Such intersubjective positioning and alignment can be a force for disruption and change. For example, it can be used to draw others into the negotiation of resistant and transformative subject positions, as where a group of contributors to 'Your identity as a mother' collectively resist being positioned as 'child-centric mothers', or contributors to 'Can we have a child exchange?' collectively construct and subvert the subject position of the 'good mother'. At moments like these, positioning themselves as members of a collective alliance means that Mumsnet users can draw on the discursive force of the entire Mumsnet community as they work to negotiate, resist or subvert dominant discourses of gendered parenthood. When they adopt such a collective position, their voices can become very powerful in this local context. The drive to align with others and adopt a shared position as a member of the Mumsnet 'in-group', however, can also work to reinforce the status quo – for example where the established substitution of the words 'child' and 'husband' with the acronyms 'DC' and 'DH' works to fix family relations as exclusively loving bonds. In 'Can we have a child exchange?', we saw that the collaborative construction and subversion of the 'good mother' subject position may be ironic and subversive, but it also reinforces the dominance of socio-cultural expectations around 'good' motherhood and makes it difficult for diverse voices to be heard.

Despite the opportunities for play, resistance and subversion in Mumsnet Talk interactions, the explorations of both this and the previous chapter show that discourses of gendered parenthood persistently work to position Mumsnet users in restrictive subject positions. At the start of Chapter 5, I showed that contributors to 'Your identity as a mother' and 'Can we have a child exchange?' are positioned within a discourse of 'gendered parenthood' through direct and indirect gendered indices. I also pointed out that the title of the Mumsnet website itself reinforces the common-sense legitimacy of the gendered subject position 'mum' across the site, working to limit the subject positions available to its members. Mumsnet users are rarely able to completely escape this subject position or the discourses that constitute it. This much is evident where contributors to 'Your identity as a mother' position themselves as individuals or as equal parents, yet also position themselves as mothers. Some resist being positioned exclusively as mothers but embrace being partially positioned in this way; others resist being positioned as the 'main parent', but the language they use to position themselves in relation to fathers nevertheless fixes them in this subject position. Where 'gendered parenthood' merges with and takes shape in discourses such as 'child-centric motherhood', 'classed motherhood' and 'commercialized motherhood', gendered parental subject positions are defined in increasingly specific and restrictive ways. For example, as I have shown both here and in Chapter 5, the 'good mother' of 'Can we have a child exchange?' is constituted through the interdiscursive relation of all four of these discourses. The analysis presented in this chapter has shown that, although contributors to 'Can we have a child exchange?' resist and subvert this subject position, they do so almost exclusively *through* their adoption of the 'good mother' subject position itself. This further points to the dominance of discourses of gendered parenthood and the difficulty for Mumsnet users to escape these discourses and the gendered parental subject positions they produce. Mumsnet users' multiple, shifting, and at times apparently contradictory self-positioning is indicative of a process of negotiation. Yet the force and persistence of dominant discourses of gendered parenthood are continually evident in their interactions.

As we move towards the close of this book, it can be said, in sum, that Mumsnet Talk cannot be singularly conceptualized as a site for either the resistance and subversion or the reproduction and approval of dominant discourses of gendered parenthood. There is certainly support to be found here for Pedersen and Smithson's (2013: 105) claim that Mumsnet Talk 'provides a forum for shifting gender norms online'. The 'Your identity as a mother' thread, indeed, is entirely devoted to the negotiation of what it means to be a 'mother', and contributors to both this thread and 'Can we have a child exchange?' can be seen at times to experiment with the subject positions available to them, such as 'parent' versus 'mother', or to emphasize the limitations of subject positions such as the 'good mother', which takes in several discourses of gendered parenthood. However, I have also shown that discourses of gendered parenthood are dominant and powerful in the context of the Mumsnet Talk threads analyzed here, persistently working to position Mumsnet users in gendered parental subject positions, even when they work to resist being positioned in this way. In the final chapter of this book, I will further detail and emphasize these key findings, as well as pointing to the wider significance and implications of the insights this book has revealed, and suggesting future avenues for research on language, gender and parenthood online.

Notes

1 The analysis that is presented in this chapter draws on, elaborates and brings together analysis and insights first introduced in Mackenzie (2017a, 2018). The section 'Negotiating child-centric motherhood' particularly relates to Mackenzie (2018), and the section 'Negotiating gendered parenthood' to Mackenzie (2017a).

2 The precise nature of 'attachment parenting' is subject to much disagreement, not least by those who are committed to it. I attempt to offer a relatively objective summary of the philosophy here, but it is no doubt influenced by my own perspectives on parenting.

3 As noted in chapters 4 and 5, all extracts from Mumsnet Talk are reproduced exactly as they are presented in the original discussions, with glosses added for acronyms. All extracts are reproduced with the permission of both the individual authors of the posts, and Mumsnet Limited. The majority of usernames are reproduced as in the original posts, but some are pseudonyms, at participants' requests.

7   Conclusion

Language, gender and parenthood online

This book's exploration of language, gender and parenthood online has revealed how women take up, negotiate and resist the cultural norms and expectations around being a woman and a parent in a popular British online discussion forum, Mumsnet Talk. Existing research on gender, parenthood and society, including that which focuses on both digital and non-digital contexts, has tended not to take the kind of rigorously theoretical approach that is presented here. Yet this book has demonstrated the continued relevance of feminist poststructuralist theory for the analysis of interactions that take place in busy, relatively unregulated digital contexts such as Mumsnet Talk. This theoretical stance has supported the identification and analysis of the multiple voices and perspectives that can be heard in this context, the identification of eight discourses of parenthood, and a detailed exploration of *how* these discourses are taken up and negotiated in digital interactions. By analyzing the operation of these discourses, this book has uncovered some of the specific ways in which parenthood is defined and understood, and some of the interactional moves that can be used to negotiate such forms of knowledge. It has revealed how a range of discourses can be drawn into the constitution of gendered parental subject positions, such as the 'mother as main parent', 'absent father' and 'good mother', thereby placing increasingly narrow and specific demands upon parents, especially women who are parents. By unpacking the multiple discursive elements in the constitution of individual subjectivity at particular moments of interaction, I have shown just how ingrained these 'common-sense' gendered parental subject positions can be.

Of the eight discourses that are named and analyzed in this book, 'gendered parenthood' is identified as the most important and pervasive. This overarching discourse works to position parents in distinct, binary subject positions – as 'mothers' and 'fathers' – even where they resist being positioned in these ways. This dominant, overarching discourse encapsulates a number of other discourses identified in the wider literature, such as 'intensive motherhood' and 'child-centricity'. Yet this is the first time that 'gendered parenthood' has been identified and specifically named as a pervasive discourse that underpins 'common-sense' meanings around gender, parenthood and raising children. Naming this discourse and specifying some of the linguistic mechanisms through which it operates therefore make a significant contribution to scholarship in the social sciences that explores the demands and expectations placed on parents, especially mothers.

Identifying and scrutinizing the operation of 'gendered parenthood' also has important implications beyond the academic context, because it can reveal some of the forms of knowledge, and ways of representing this knowledge, that limit the options available to parents. The pervasive presence of this discourse dismantles the illusion that 'parenthood' is a gender-neutral construction, and shows how difficult it can be for parents to move beyond restrictive, dichotomous gender norms, even when they have access to relatively open, egalitarian spaces like Mumsnet Talk. 'Gendered parenthood' becomes even more difficult to contest when it merges and interrelates with other discourses, such as 'mother as main parent', 'absent fathers' and 'child-centric motherhood'. The interdiscursive operation of these discourses, for example, will make it difficult for male parents to be positioned as primary carers who make substantial sacrifices for their children, or for families who fall outside of the binary parental unit of mother and father, such as single, same-sex, non-binary or kinship carers and parents, to position themselves in ways that are socially valued and legitimized.

Identifying the seven other discourses that are taken up and negotiated in Mumsnet Talk threads has revealed some of the specific ways in which parents can be positioned as gendered subjects. For example, the way the 'mother as main parent' and 'child-centric motherhood' discourses operate in Mumsnet Talk interactions shows that it is difficult for female Mumsnet users to position themselves in a way that is not related to their children. The identification of these discourses, as well as 'classed motherhood' and 'commercialized motherhood', builds upon extensive scholarship in the social sciences that points to the expectations of 'intensive' and 'good' mothers in a western context. It supports the argument that these expectations continue to be tied to essentialist notions of women's 'natural' position as self-sacrificing carers and nurturers, and that 'good' mothers have middle class values that, more recently, have been tied with consumerist practices. The identification of the 'absent fathers' discourse adds weight to the claim that fathers are marginalized in the family sphere. Indeed, I go a step further by showing how fathers can be completely excluded from this sphere, through their notable absence in both specific Mumsnet Talk threads and the forum more generally. Two final discourses, 'equal parenting' and 'individuality', are identified as sites for the resistance and negotiation of discourses of gendered parenthood, showing that Mumsnet Talk is a space in which dominant norms of gender and parenthood can be challenged. Nevertheless, analysis of the way these discourses are taken up in Mumsnet Talk interactions shows that gender is still foregrounded in their construction, where non-gendered subject positions such as 'parent' and 'me' are frequently taken up in opposition to the gendered subject position 'mother'. The oppositional construction of these subject positions shows just how much discourses of gendered parenthood suffuse the constitution of parental subjectivities in Mumsnet Talk, even where they may seem, at first glance, to be relatively gender-neutral.

Despite underlining the dominance of discourses of gendered parenthood, this book has also shown that contributors to Mumsnet Talk are able to negotiate these discourses, and to take up subject positions that may be subversive or transformative in nature. This forum, like many other community-based platforms, seems to engender social and linguistic innovation, flexibility and openness amongst its users, thereby opening up spaces for the negotiation and contestation of dominant forms of knowledge and subjectivity. I have particularly emphasized the importance of collaborative and intersubjective alignment within Mumsnet Talk, showing that contributors' use of in-group resources, such as distinctive acronyms and reliance on 'insider' knowledge, allows them to draw on a collective voice that can both empower them in this local context and strengthen their resistance to dominant norms. However, I have also suggested that these interactional norms can constrain users' access to diverse subject positions and forms of expression, as where certain acronyms can work to fix the positioning of family members, such as (darling) husbands, partners and children, in particular ways.

In short, this book has shown that negotiating motherhood online is a complex interaction between individual autonomy, dominant discourses and local norms of sharing and interaction. Its balanced consideration of these elements distinguishes it from previous studies of gender and parenthood in a range of contexts, including those that focus on the digital. I have shown that sites like Mumsnet are places where ordinary people have the opportunity to negotiate and discuss wider social constructs such as 'motherhood', and thus may be key initiators of resistance, change and transformation. However, digital technologies and affordances do not necessarily allow their users to transcend social forces, or to escape the language through which they operate. The power of dominant discourses to position individuals in restrictive ways, and the difficulty of evading these discourses, means that even when individuals are able to be particularly open and innovative in their interactions, they are still subject to the same discursive constraints. It therefore remains difficult within Mumsnet Talk, as elsewhere, for women to escape dominant discourses that work to fix them in restricted gendered subject positions. Mumsnet users' frustration at being unable to escape such positions, especially the 'good' and 'child-centric' mother, is a clear and important sign that there is a need for further research in the area of language, gender and parenthood, online and elsewhere.

I close this book with a call for further research that explores constructions of parenthood in a wider range of contexts, and by different kinds of families. It has become apparent through the exploration of Mumsnet Talk presented here that there are a number of groups who are relatively marginalized in this space, such as fathers, same-sex parents and working class parents. Whilst it is important to highlight the ways in which these groups are excluded from popular, well-known sites in which parenthood is constructed and negotiated, it is also important that a wider range of parental voices and perspectives be heard, in order to understand the multiple ways in which it is possible to be a parent in a contemporary context. There is also a growing need to explore how the pervasive, overarching dominant discourse of 'gendered parenthood' affects families who fall outside of the binary parental unit of mother and father, such as single, same-sex, non-binary or kinship carers and parents. Such explorations will be able to offer further valuable insights into the ways in which caring and parental identities are constructed, legitimized and valued in society. Interactions within digital contexts provide fruitful sites for such explorations, and the approach that is presented in this book offers an excellent starting point for the sensitive and nuanced analysis of these interactions. Through grounded, theoretical and self-reflexive explorations of language, gender and parenthood online, researchers will be well placed to explore parenthood as a site of conflict for both the individual and wider society, identify practices at the forefront of social change, and work to support individuals' access to the full spectrum of ways in which it is possible to be valued, legitimized and understood as a parent.

References

Abercrombie, N. and Warde, A. (2003) *Contemporary British Society*. Third Edn. Cambridge: Polity Press.

Agar, M. (1995) 'Ethnography', in Verschueren, J., Ostman, J. O. and Blommaert, J. (eds) *Handbook of Pragmatics Online*. Amsterdam and Philadelphia: John Benjamins Publishing Company.

Agha, A. (2007) *Language and Social Relations*. Cambridge: Cambridge University Press.

Ainsworth, M. D. S. and Bowlby, J. (1991) 'An ethological approach to personality development', *American Psychologist*, 47, pp. 331–341.

Althusser, L. (1971) 'Ideology and ideological state apparatuses', in Althusser, L. (ed.) *Lenin and Philosophy and Other Essays*. New York: Monthly Review Press, pp. 127–186.

Androutsopoulos, J. (2006) 'Multilingualism, diaspora, and the Internet: Codes and identities on German-based diaspora websites', *Journal of Sociolinguistics*, 10(4), pp. 520–547.

Androutsopoulos, J. (2008) 'Potentials and limitations of discourse-centred online ethnography', *Language@Internet*, 5, article 9.

Baker, P. (2008) *Sexed Texts: Language, Gender and Sexuality*. London: Equinox.

Bakhtin, M. (1981) *The Dialogic Imagination: Four Essays* (Holquist, M. ed. and trans.). Austin: The University of Texas Press.

Bakhtin, M. (1984 [1963]) *Problems of Dostoevsky's Poetics* (Emerson, C. ed. and trans.). Minneapolis: University of Minnesota.

Barton, D. and Lee, C. (2013) *Language Online: Investigating Digital Texts and Practices*. London: Routledge.

Bateson, G. (1972) 'A theory of play and fantasy', in Bateson, G. (ed.) *Steps to an Ecology of Mind: Collected Essays in Anthropology, Evolution and Epistemology*. London: Jason Aronson, pp. 183–198.

Baxter, J. (2003) *Positioning Gender in Discourse: A Feminist Methodology*. Basingstoke: Palgrave Macmillan.

Baxter, J. (2010) 'Discourse-analytic approaches to text and talk', in Litosseliti, L. (ed.) *Research Methods in Linguistics*. London: Continuum, pp. 117–137.

Baxter, J. (2014) *Double-Voicing at Work: Power, Gender and Linguistic Expertise*. New York: Palgrave Macmillan.

Bazeley, P. (2007) *Qualitative Data Analysis with NVivo*. London: Sage.

Benwell, B. and Stokoe, E. (2006) *Discourse and Identity*. Edinburgh: Edinburgh University Press.

Bhatia, V. (2005) 'Generic patterns in promotional discourse', in Halmari, H. and Virtanen, T. (eds) *Persuasion Across Genres: A Linguistic Approach*. Amsterdam and Philadelphia: John Benjamins Publishing Company, pp. 213–228.

Boon, S. and Pentney, B. (2015) 'Virtual lactivism: Breastfeeding selfies and the performance of motherhood', *International Journal of Communication*, 9, pp. 1759–1774.

Bourdieu, P. (1984) *Distinction: A Social Critique of the Judgement of Taste* (Nice, R. ed.). London: Routledge.

Bowlby, J. (1969) *Attachment and Loss, Vol. 1: Attachment*. New York: Basic Books.

Brady, E. and Guerin, S. (2010) ' "Not the romantic, all happy, coochy coo experience": A qualitative analysis of interactions on an Irish parenting web site', *Family Relations*, 59(1), pp. 14–27.

Bruns, A. (2008) *Blogs, Wikipedia, Second Life and Beyond: From Production to Produsage*. Berlin: Peter Lang.

Bucholtz, M. (2009) 'From stance to style: Gender, interaction, and indexicality in Mexican immigrant youth slang', in Jaffe, A. (ed.) *Stance: Sociolinguistic Perspectives*. New York: Oxford University Press, pp. 146–170.

Butler, C. (2002) *Postmodernism: A Very Short Introduction*. Oxford: Oxford University Press.

Cameron, D. (1996) 'The language-gender interface: Challenging co-optation', in Bing, J. M., Bergvall, V. L. and Freed, A. F. (eds) *Rethinking Language and Gender Research: Theory and Practice*. London: Longman, pp. 31–53.

Cameron, D. and Coates, J. (1989) 'Some problems in the sociolinguistic explanation of sex differences', in Coates, J. and Cameron, D. (eds) *Women in Their Speech Communities*. London: Longman, pp. 13–26.

Chan, A. H. N. (2008) ' "Life in Happy Land": Using virtual space and doing motherhood in Hong Kong', *Gender, Place & Culture*, 15(2), pp. 169–188.

Charmaz, K. (2008) 'Grounded theory in the 21st century: Applications for advancing social justice studies', in Denzin, N. K. and Lincoln, Y. S. (eds) *Strategies of Qualitative Inquiry*. Third Edn. Los Angeles: Sage, pp. 203–242.

Charmaz, K. (2014) *Constructing Grounded Theory*. Second Edn. Los Angeles: Sage.

Charmaz, K. and Bryant, A. (2011) 'Grounded theory and credibility', in Silverman, D. (ed.) *Qualitative Research: Theory, Method and Practice*. Third Edn. London: Sage, pp. 291–309.

Cherny, L. (1999) *Conversation and Community: Chat in a Virtual World*. Stanford, CA: CSLI Publications.

Clarke, A. E. (2003) 'Situational analyses: Grounded theory mapping after the postmodern turn', *Symbolic Interaction*, 26(4), pp. 553–576.

Coates, J. (1988) 'Gossip revisited: Language in all-female groups', in Coates, J. and Cameron, D. (eds) *Women in Their Speech Communities*. London: Longman, pp. 94–121.

Coates, J. (1996) *Women Talk: Conversation Between Women Friends*. Oxford: Blackwell Publishers Ltd.

Collins, P. H. and Bilge, S. (2016) *Intersectionality*. Cambridge: Polity Press.

Corbin, J. and Strauss, A. (2008) *Basics of Qualitative Research: Techniques and Procedures for Developing Grounded Theory*. Third Edn. London: Sage.

Cormode, G. and Krishnamurthy, B. (2008) 'Key differences between Web 1.0 and Web 2.0', *First Monday*, 13(6).

Danet, B. (2001) *Cyberpl@y: Communicating Online*. Oxford: Berg.

Danet, B., Ruedenberg-Wright, L. and Rosenbaum-Tamari, Y. (1997) ' "Hmmm . . . Where's that smoke coming from?" Writing, play and performance on Internet Relay Chat', *Journal of Computer-Mediated Communication*, 2(4).

Davies, B. and Harré, R. (1990) 'Positioning: The discursive production of selves', *Journal for the Theory of Social Behaviour*, 20(1), pp. 43–46.

Denzin, N. K. and Lincoln, Y. S. (2008) *Strategies of Qualitative Inquiry*. Third Edn. Los Angeles: Sage.

Dey, I. (1993) *Qualitative Data Analysis: A User-Friendly Guide for Social Scientists*. London: Routledge.

Dörnyei, Z. (2007) *Research Methods in Applied Linguistics: Quantitative, Qualitative and Mixed Methodologies*. Oxford: Oxford University Press.

Du Bois, J. W. (2007) 'The stance triangle', in Englebretson, R. (ed.) *Stancetaking in Discourse: Subjectivity, Evaluation, Interaction*. Amsterdam: Benjamins, pp. 139–182.

Du Bois, J. W. (2014) 'Towards a dialogic syntax', *Cognitive Linguistics*, 25(3), pp. 359–410.

Duerden, N. (2013) 'Why has Mumsnet developed such an awkward reputation?', *The Independent*, May 11th. Available at: www.independent.co.uk/life-style.

Eckert, P. and McConnell-Ginet, S. (1992) 'Communities of practice: Where language, gender, and power all live', in Hall, K., Bucholtz, M., and Moonwomon, B. (eds) *Locating Power: Proceedings of the 1992 Berkeley Women and Language Conference*. Berkeley: Berkeley Women and Language Group, pp. 89–99.

Edmondson, N. (2012) 'Fathers 4 Justice Stage Naked Mumsnet Protest in Marks & Spencer Oxford Street', *International Business Times Online*, March 19th. Available at: www.ibtimes.co.uk/articles

Elm, M. S. (2007) 'Doing and undoing gender in a Swedish internet community', in Elm, M. S. and Sundén, J. (eds) *Cyberfeminism in Northern Lights: Digital Media and Gender in a Nordic Context*. Newcastle: Cambridge Scholars Publishing, pp. 104–129.

Ennis, L. R. (2014) *Intensive Mothering: The Cultural Contradictions of Modern Motherhood*. Toronto: Demeter Press.

Ess, C. (2007) 'Internet research ethics', in Fossheim, H. and Ingierd, H. (eds) *The Oxford Handbook of Internet Psychology*. New York: Oxford University Press, pp. 487–502.

Fairclough, N. (1992) *Discourse and Social Change*. Cambridge: Polity Press.

Fischer, J. and Anderson, V. N. (2012) 'Gender role attitudes and characteristics of stay-at-home and employed fathers', *Psychology of Men & Masculinity*, 13(1), pp. 16–31.

Fishman, P. (1983) 'Interaction: The work women do', in Thorne, B., Kramarae, C. and Henley, N. (eds) *Language, Gender and Society*. Rowley, MA: Newbury House, pp. 89–101.

Foucault, M. (1972) *The Archaeology of Knowledge* (Sheridan Smith, A. M. ed.). London: Routledge.

Foucault, M. (1978) *The History of Sexuality Volume 1: An Introduction* (Hurley, R. ed.). London: Penguin.

Fought, C. (2006) *Language and Ethnicity*. Cambridge: Cambridge University Press.

Garcia, A. C. and Jacobs, J. B. (1999) 'The eyes of the beholder: Understanding the turn-taking system in quasi-synchronous computer-mediated communication', *Research on Language and Social Interaction*, 32(4), pp. 337–367.

Georgakopoulou, A. (2005) 'Computer-mediated communication', in Verschueren, J. et al. (eds) *Handbook of Pragmatics Online*. Amsterdam and Philadelphia: John Benjamins Publishing Company.

Gibbs, G. R. (2002) *Qualitative Data Analysis: Explorations with NVivo*. Philadelphia: Open University Press.

Gibson, J. (1977) 'The theory of affordances', in Shaw, R. and Bransford, J. (eds) *Perceiving, Acting, and Knowing*. Hillsdale: Lawrence Erlbaum, pp. 67–82.

Giddens, A. (1981) *The Class Structure of the Advanced Societies*. Second Edn. London: Hutchinson University Library.

Gill, R. (1995) 'Relativism, reflexivity and politics: Interrogating discourse analysis from a feminist perspective', in Wilkinson, S. and Kitzinger, C. (eds) *Feminism and Discourse: Psychological Perspectives*. London: Sage, pp. 165–186.

Gillies, V. (2007) *Marginalised Mothers: Exploring Working Class Experiences of Parenting*. Oxon: Routledge.

Glaser, B. G. and Strauss, A. L. (1967) *The Discovery of Grounded Theory: Strategies for Qualitative Research*. Chicago: Aldine.

Goffman, E. (1974) *Frame Analysis: An Essay on the Organization of Experience*. Boston: Northeastern University Press.

Gold, R. L. (1958) 'Roles in sociological field observations', *Social Forces*, 36(3), pp. 217–223.

Goldthorpe, J. H. (1980) *Social Mobility and Class Structure in Modern Britain*. Oxford: Clarendon Press.

Gong, Y. (2016) 'Online discourse of masculinities in transnational football fandom: Chinese Arsenal fans' talk around "gaofushuai" and "diaosi" ', *Discourse & Society*, 27(1), pp. 20–37.

Graham, L. J. (2005) 'Discourse analysis and the critical use of Foucault', Australian Association for Research in Education, 2005 Annual Conference, Sydney, pp. 1–15.

Green, J. L. and Bloome, D. (1997) 'Ethnography and ethnographers of and in education: A situated perspective', in Flood, J., Heath, S. B. and Lapp, D. (eds) *Handbook for Literacy Educators: Research in the Community and Visual Arts*. New York: Palgrave Macmillan, pp. 181–202.

Hall, M., Gough, B., Seymour-Smith, S. and Henson, S. (2012) 'On-line constructions of metrosexuality and masculinities: A membership categorization analysis', *Gender and Language*, 6(2), pp. 379–404.

Halonen, M. and Leppänen, S. (2017) ' "Pissis stories": Performing transgressive and precarious girlhood in social media', in Leppänen, S., Westinen, S. and Kytölä, S. (eds) *Social Media Discourse, (Dis)identifications and Diversities*. New York: Routledge, pp. 39–61.

Hammersley, M. and Atkinson, P. (2007) *Ethnography: Principles in Practice.* Third Edn. London: Routledge.

Handelman, D. (1977) 'Play and ritual: Complementary frames of meta-communication', in Chapman, A. and Foot, H. (eds) *It's a Funny Thing, Humour.* Oxford, New York, Toronto, Sydney, Paris, Frankfurt: Pergamon Press, pp. 185–192.

Hanell, L. and Salö, L. (2017) 'Nine months of entextualizations: Discourse and knowledge in an online discussion forum thread for expectant parents', in Kerfoot, C. and Hyltenstam, K. (eds) *Entangled Discourses: South-North Orders of Visibility*, New York: Routledge, pp. 154–170.

Hays, S. (1996) *The Cultural Contradictions of Motherhood.* New Haven: Yale University Press.

Herring, S. C. and Androutsopoulos, J. (2015) 'Computer-mediated discourse 2.0', in Tannen, D., Hamilton, H. E. and Schiffrin, D. (eds) *The Handbook of Discourse Analysis.* Second Edn. Oxford: John Wiley & Sons, pp. 127–151.

Hine, C. (2000) *Virtual Ethnography.* London: Sage.

Hine, C. (2009) 'How can qualitative internet researchers define the boundaries of their projects?', in Markham, A. N. and Baym, N. K. (eds) *Internet Inquiry: Conversations About Method.* Los Angeles: Sage, pp. 1–20.

Holmes, J. (1984) 'Hedging your bets and sitting on the fence: Some evidence for hedges as support structures', *Te Reo*, 27, pp. 47–62.

Holmes, J. and Stubbe, M. (2003) ' "Feminine" workplaces: Stereotype and reality', in Holmes, J. and Meyerhoff, M. (eds) *The Handbook of Language and Gender.* Oxford: Blackwell Publishing, pp. 573–600.

Jäger, S. and Maier, F. (2009) 'Theoretical and methodological aspects of Foucauldian critical discourse analysis and dispositive analysis', in Wodak, R. and Meyer, M. (eds) *Methods of Critical Discourse Analysis.* Second Edn. London: Sage, pp. 34–61.

Jäntti, S., Saresma, T., Leppänen, S., Järvinen, S. and Varis, P. (2017) 'Homing blogs as ambivalent spaces for feminine agency', *Feminist Media Studies*, 18(1), https://doi.org/10.1080/14680777.2017.1396234

Jaworska, S. (2017) ' "Bad" mums and the "untellable": Narrative practices and agency in online stories about postnatal depression on Mumsnet'. *Discourse, Context & Media.* Available at: www.sciencedirect.com/science/article/pii/S221169581730137X.

Jensen, T. (2013) ' "Mumsnetiquette": Online affect within parenting culture', in Maxwell, C. and Aggleton, P. (eds) *Privilege, Agency and Affect: Understanding the Production and Effects of Action.* Basingstoke: Palgrave Macmillan, pp. 127–145.

Johnston, D. D. and Swanson, D. H. (2006) 'Constructing the "good mother": The experience of mothering ideologies by work status', *Sex Roles*, 54(7–8), pp. 509–519.

Johnston, D. D. and Swanson, D. H. (2007) 'Cognitive acrobatics in the construction of worker – mother identity', *Sex Roles*, 57(5–6), pp. 447–459.

Johnstone, B. and Kiesling, S. F. (2008) 'Indexicality and experience: Exploring the meanings of /aw/ – monopthongization in Pittsburgh', *Journal of Sociolinguistics*, 12(1), pp. 5–33.

Jones, L. (2018) 'I'm not proud, I'm just gay: Lesbian and gay youths' discursive negotiation of otherness', *Journal of Sociolinguistics*, 22(1), pp. 55–76.

Jule, A. (2008) *A Beginner's Guide to Language and Gender*. Cleveland: Multilingual Matters.

Lakoff, R. (1975) *Language and Woman's Place*. New York: Harper Torch.

Lawler, S. (2000) *Mothering the Self: Mothers, Daughters, Subjects*. London: Routledge.

Lehtonen, S. (2017) ' "I just don't know what went wrong": Neo-sincerity and doing gender and age otherwise in a discussion forum for Finnish fans of My Little Pony', in Leppänen, S., Westinen, E. and Kytölä, S. (eds) *Social Media Discourse, (Dis)identifications and Diversities*. New York: Routledge, pp. 287–309.

Leppänen, S. (2008) 'Cybergirls in trouble? Fan fiction as a discursive space for interrogating gender and sexuality', in Caldas-Coulthard, C. M. and Iedema, R. (eds) *Identity Trouble: Critical Discourse and Contested Identities*. Basingstoke: Palgrave Macmillan, pp. 156–179.

Leppänen, S. and Kytölä, S. (2017) 'Investigating multilingualism and multisemioticity as communicative resources in social media', in Martin-Jones, M. and Martin, D. (eds) *Researching Multilingualism: Critical and Ethnographic Perspectives*. London: Routledge, pp. 155–171.

Lowe, P. (2016) *Reproductive Health and Maternal Sacrifice: Women, Choice and Responsibility*. London: Palgrave Macmillan.

Mackenzie, J. (2017a) ' "Can we have a child exchange?" Constructing and subverting the "good mother" through play in Mumsnet Talk', *Discourse & Society*, 28(3), pp. 296–312.

Mackenzie, J. (2017b) 'Identifying informational norms in Mumsnet Talk: A reflexive-linguistic approach to internet research ethics', *Applied Linguistics Review*, 8(2–3), pp. 293–314.

Mackenzie, J. (2018) ' "Good mums don't, apparently, wear make-up": Negotiating discourses of gendered parenthood in Mumsnet Talk', *Gender and Language*, 12(1), pp. 114–135.

Madge, C. and O'Connor, H. (2006) 'Parenting gone wired: Empowerment of new mothers on the Internet?', *Social & Cultural Geography*, 7(2), pp. 199–220.

Markham, A. (2004) 'Internet communication as a tool for qualitative research', in Silverman, D. (ed.) *Qualitative Research: Theory, Method and Practice*. London: Sage, pp. 95–124.

Markham, A. (2013) 'Undermining "data": A critical examination of a core term in scientific inquiry', *First Monday*, 18(10).

Markham, A. and Buchanan, E. (2015) 'Internet research: Ethical concerns', in Wright, J. D. (ed.) *International Encyclopedia of the Social and Behavioral Sciences*. Second Edn. Amsterdam, Oxford: Elsevier, pp. 603–613.

Markham, A., Buchanan, E. and The AoIR (Association of Internet Researchers) ethics working committee. (2012) 'Ethical decision-making and Internet research: Recommendations from the AoIR ethics working committee (Version 2.0)'. Available at: http://aoir.org/reports/ethics2.pdf.

Mason, J. (2002) *Qualitative Researching*. Second Edn. London: Sage.

Mason, M. (2010) 'Sample size and saturation in PhD studies using qualitative interviews', *Forum: Qualitative Social Research*, 11(3), article 8.

McElvoy, A. (2010) 'Mumsnet has expanded into an 850,000-strong organisation and is now set to wield real clout in the election campaign', *The Scotsman*, March 7th. Available at: www.scotsman.com/news.

McVeigh, T. (2012) 'Mumsnet bloggers converge on London', *The Observer*, November 10th. Available at: www.guardian.co.uk/media.

Milani, T. M. (2013) 'Are "queers" really "queer"? Language, identity and same-sex desire in a South African online community', *Discourse & Society*, 24(5), pp. 615–633.

Miller, T. (2007) ' "Is this what motherhood is all about?" Weaving experiences and discourse through transition to first-time motherhood', *Gender & Society*, 21(3), pp. 337–358.

Miller, T. (2011) 'Falling back into gender? Men's narratives and practices around first-time fatherhood', *Sociology*, 45(6), pp. 1094–1109.

Mills, S. and Mullany, L. (2011) *Language, Gender and Feminism: Theory, Methodology and Practice*. London: Routledge.

Moravec, M. (2011) 'Expectant motherhood: How online communities shape pregnancy', in Moravec, M. (ed.) *Motherhood Online*. Newcastle upon Tyne: Cambridge Scholars Publishing, pp. 2–22.

Mulcahy, C. C., Parry, D. C. and Glover, T. D. (2015) 'From mothering without a net to mothering on the net: The impact of an online social networking site on experiences of postpartum depression', *Journal of the Motherhood Initiative for Research and Community Involvement*, 6(1), pp. 92–106.

Mumsnet Limited (2017) Available at: www.mumsnet.com/.

Ochs, E. (1992) 'Indexing gender', in Duranti, A. and Goodwin, C. (eds) *Rethinking Context: Language as an Interactive Phenomenon*. Cambridge: Cambridge University Press, pp. 335–358.

Page, R., Barton, D., Unger, J. W. and Zappavigna, M. (2014) *Researching Language and Social Media: A Student Guide*. London: Routledge.

Parkin, F. (1971) *Class Inequality and Political Order*. London: MacGibbon and Kee.

Pedersen, S. (2016) 'The good, the bad and the "good enough" mother on the UK parenting forum Mumsnet', *Women's Studies International Forum*, 59, pp. 32–38.

Pedersen, S. and Smithson, J. (2010) 'Membership and activity in an online parenting community', in Taiwo, R. (ed.) *Handbook of Research on Discourse Behavior and Digital Communication: Language Structures and Social Interaction*. New York: Information Science Reference, vol. 1, pp. 88–103.

Pedersen, S. and Smithson, J. (2013) 'Mothers with attitude – how the Mumsnet parenting forum offers space for new forms of femininity to emerge online', *Women's Studies International Forum*, 38, pp. 97–106.

Reisigl, M. and Wodak, R. (2009) 'The discourse-historical approach (DHA)', in Wodak, R. and Meyer, M. (eds) *Methods of Critical Discourse Analysis*. Second Edn. London: Sage, pp. 87–121.

Rellstab, D. H. (2007) 'Staging gender online: Gender plays in Swiss internet relay chats', *Discourse & Society*, 18(6), pp. 765–787.

Robson, C. (2011) *Real World Research: A Resource for Users of Social Research Methods in Applied Settings*. Third Edn. Chichester: John Wiley & Sons.

Rüdiger, S. and Dayter, D. (2017) 'The ethics of researching unlikeable subjects', *Applied Linguistics Review*, 8(2–3), pp. 251–269.

Saussure, F. de (1974) *Course in General Linguistics* (Bally, C. et al. ed.). Third Edn. New York: McGraw-Hill Book Company.

Savage, M. Cunningham, N., Devine, F., Friedman, S., Laurison, D., Mckenzie, L., Miles, A., Snee, H. and Wakeling, H. (2015) *Social Class in the 21st Century*. London: Pelican.

Seargeant, P. and Tagg, C. (2014) 'Introduction: The language of social media', in Seargeant, P. and Tagg, C. (eds) *The Language of Social Media*. New York: Palgrave Macmillan, pp. 1–20.

Sears, W. and Sears, M. (2003) *The Baby Book: Everything You Need to Know About Your Baby From Birth to Age Two*. Second Edn. New York: Little, Brown and Co.

Sibary, S. (2013) 'Why I hate the smug bullies on Mumsnet!', *The Mail Online*, April 11th. Available at: www.dailymail.co.uk/femail.

Silverman, D. (2011) *Qualitative Research: Issues of Theory, Method and Practice*. Third Edn. Los Angeles: Sage.

Skeggs, B. (1997) *Formations of Class and Gender: Becoming Respectable*. London: Sage.

Spilioti, T. (2017) 'Media convergence and publicness: Towards a modular and iterative approach to online research ethics', *Applied Linguistics Review*, 8(2–3), pp. 191–212.

Strauss, A. L. and Corbin, J. M. (1998) *Basics of Qualitative Research: Techniques and Procedures for Developing Grounded Theory*. Third Edn. London: Sage.

Sunderland, J. (2000) 'Baby entertainer, bumbling assistant and line manager: Discourses of fatherhood in parentcraft texts', *Discourse & Society*, 11(2), pp. 249–274.

Sunderland, J. (2004) *Gendered Discourses*. New York: Palgrave Macmillan.

Sunstein, C. R. (2001) *Republic.com 2.0*. Princeton: Princeton University Press.

Sveningsson Elm, M. (2009) 'How do various notions of privacy influence decisions in qualitative internet research?', in Markham, A. and Baym, N. (eds) *Internet Inquiry: Conversations About Method*. Los Angeles: Sage, pp. 69–87.

Takševa, T. (2014) 'How contemporary consumerism shapes intensive mothering practices', in Ennis, L. R. (ed.) *Intensive Mothering: The Cultural Contradictions of Modern Motherhood*. Toronto: Demeter Press, pp. 211–232.

Tannen, D. (2007) *Talking Voices: Repetition, Dialogue, and Imagery in Conversational Discourse*. Second Edn. Cambridge: Cambridge University Press.

Thelwall, M. and Wilkinson, D. (2010) 'Researching personal information on the public web: Methods and ethics', *Social Science Computer Review*, 29(4), pp. 387–401.

Thurlow, C. (2013) 'Facebook: Synthetic media, pseudo-sociality, and the rhetorics of Web 2.0', in Tannen, D. and Trester, A. (eds) *Discourse 2.0. Language and New Media*. Washington, DC: Georgetown University Press, pp. 225–250.

Turkle, S. (1995) *Life on the Screen*. New York: Simon & Schuster Paperbacks.

Vaisman, C. (2013) 'Beautiful script, cute spelling and glamorous words: Doing girlhood through language playfulness on Israeli blogs', *Language & Communication*, 34, pp. 69–80.

Van Dijck, J. (2013) *The Culture of Connectivity: A Critical History of Social Media*. Oxford: Oxford University Press.

Van Leeuwen, T. (1995) 'Representing social action', *Discourse & Society*, 6(1), pp. 81–106.

Van Leeuwen, T. (1996) 'The representation of social actors', in Caldas-Coulthard, C. and Coulthard, M. (eds) *Texts and Practices: Readings in Critical Discourse Analysis*. London: Routledge, pp. 32–70.

Van Leeuwen, T. (2009) 'Discourse as the recontextualization of social practice: A guide', in Wodak, R. and Meyer, M. (eds) *Methods of Critical Discourse Analysis*. Second Edn. Los Angeles: Sage, pp. 144–161.

Wall, G. (2010) 'Mothers' experiences with intensive parenting and brain development discourse', *Women's Studies International Forum*, 33(3), pp. 253–263.

Wall, G. (2013) '"Putting family first": Shifting discourses of motherhood and childhood in representations of mothers' employment and child care', *Women's Studies International Forum*, 40, pp. 162–171.

Weedon, C. (1997) *Feminist Practice and Poststructuralist Theory*. Second Edn. Oxford: Blackwell Publishing.

Wolf, A. (2000) 'Emotional expression online: Gender differences in emoticon use', *Cyberpsychology & Behaviour*, 3(5), pp. 827–833.

Worthington, N. (2005) 'Women's work on the World Wide Web: How a new medium represents an old problem', *Popular Communication*, 3(1), pp. 43–60.

Zappavigna, M. (2012). *Discourse of Twitter and Social Media*. London: Continuum.

Zimman, L. (2014) 'The discursive construction of sex', in Zimman, L., Davis, J. and Raclaw, J. (eds) *Queer Excursions: Retheorizing Binaries in Language and Sexuality*. Oxford: Oxford University Press, pp. 14–34.

Index

parody 21, 22, 99, 101; *see also*
    humour; irony; play
'part-time father' discourse 13, 16, 17, 62
patriarchy 7–8
play 20, 22, 23, 25, 45, 60, 61, 71, 74,
    78, 96, 99, 101, 102, 103; *see also*
    humour; irony; parody
positioning theory 49, 90, 96
postmodernism 8
poststructuralism 7–9, 14, 15, 17, 19,
    33, 35, 51
power 8–11, 14, 17, 57, 90, 99, 101
pragmatic research 31
produsers 23
pronouns 6–7, 59, 63, 64, 65, 68, 70,
    81, 84, 86
public: online site 3, 21, 27; *versus*
    private 37, 52
purposive sampling 37–38

qualitative data analysis software
    42–43
qualitative research 30–31, 33, 35

regulation 9, 10; discursive 10; social
    3; *see also* regulatory
regulatory: forces 14; frameworks 9;
    practices 4; statements 9
repetition 16, 51, 59, 95; recurrence
    and 16
resistance 1, 7, 8, 9, 29, 33, 44, 51–52,
    69, 80, 84, 85, 87, 93–94, 96, 99,
    103–104, 106, 107, 108

same-sex parents *see* parent
sampling *see* purposive sampling
saturation 43
Saussure, F. de. 8, 118
self-reflexivity 33, 35, 37, 42,
    109
significant moment 48–49, 89–90
single parents *see* parent
single-voicing 50
stance triangle 51
stereotypes *see* femininity; masculinity;
    motherhood
strikethrough text 25, 26, 75,
    96, 100
subjectivity 10, 17, 48, 49, 90
subject positions 4, 5, 10, 11, 48, 58,
    59, 86, 89, 102–104, 108; *see also*
    common sense; father; mother;
    parent
subversion *see* resistance
Sunderland, J. 3, 11–17, 30, 46, 61, 62,
    66–67, 118

thematic codes *see* coding
theoretical codes *see* coding
threads 6–7, 21, 23–24, 43–45;
    collection 34–35, 39; sampling
    37–38
transformative: meanings 4, 9;
    moments 6–7; potential 36; practices
    22, 27, 89, 102–103, 108

Weedon, C. 8, 9, 10, 119

Die Deutsche Bibliothek CIP-Einheitsaufnahme ... ...
Ein Titeldatensatz für diese Publikation ist bei Der Deutschen Bibliothek erhältlich.
Verlag GmbH, Konfigurations str. 24, 50411 Musterhausen/Germany